Vittorio Se~~

ENCHANT~~G

FLORENCE

**THE CHURCHES • THE MUSEUMS • THE MONUMENTS
THE PALACES • THE GARDENS • FIESOLE AND OTHER
LOCATIONS IN 8 STREET BY STREET ITINERARIES**

★ 250 Colour Illustrations
★ Map of the town

BONECHI EDIZIONI «IL TURISMO» - FIRENZE

© Copyright 1989 by Bonechi Edizioni "Il Turismo" S.r.l.
© Copyright 2000 by Bonechi Edizioni "Il Turismo" S.r.l.
Via dei Rustici, 5 - 50122 FLORENCE
Tel. +39-055 239.82.24/25 - Fax +39-055 21.63.66
E-mail address: barbara@bonechi.com
                bbonechi@dada.it
http://www.bonechi.com
Printed in Italy

Photos: Bonechi Edizioni "Il Turismo" S.r.l. Archives
Photos of recently restored or rearranged items: Studio C.D.;
Antonio de Magistris; Arold Spindles; Piero Bonechi; Rolando Fusi.
Graphs and floor-plans: editorial staff
Maps: Bonechi Edizioni "Il Turismo" S.r.l., Florence
Lay-out and cover: Claudia Baggiani
English version revised by: Rosalynd C. Pio
Coordination: Barbara Bonechi
Print: BO.BA.DO.MA., Florence
ISBN 88-7204-279-8

HISTORICAL NOTE

The origins of Florence are lost in time. The Etruscans probably founded a small settlement inhabited chiefly by boatmen and fishermen down near the river, but it was only under Roman sway, around the middle of the 1st century B.C. that "Florentia" became a proper town, situated like a number of other Roman centres along the fertile banks of a river, the Arno, in this case. The valley site encouraged agricultural and commercial development and the little Roman town throve and flourished, living up to its Latin name (Florentia means flowering). Florentia possessed temples, baths, an amphitheatre, a Capitol or building for the governing assembly (Campidoglio), like any Roman town of its time. A number of street names (e.g.: Via delle Terme, Via del Campidoglio, etc.) recall the sites of these buildings. Two thoroughfares running from east to west (the decumanus) and from north to south (the cardus) divided the town into four quarters. These "guidelines" would be respected in the centuries to come when the medieval town grew-up upon its Roman foundations. The advent of Christianity brought many new buildings with it, such as Santa Felicita, Santa Reparata, San Lorenzo, etc., which date back to the earliest Christian centuries. Charlemagne came to stay in the town, in the 8th century. Over the following centuries, up to the 11th, when the town claimed the status of Free Commune for itself, it was ruled over by a succession of counts, barons, and feudal lords of various origins, until at last the second circle of walls was built in 1073. The first major expansion occurred after the year 1000: the Baptistery, San Miniato al Monte, Santissimi Apostoli, Santo Stefano and other great Romanesque buildings were all constructed in the 11th century. During the 12th and 13th centuries, the population of approximately 60,000 people (at the time London numbered less than half) was busily engaged in trade with nearly every Mediterranean port. Two industries, wool and silk were responsible for the city's incredible commercial success. Rough silk from Asia and uncarded wool from all over Europe were shipped to Florence via the port of Pisa, to be carded, woven and dyed-by the Florentines who employed secret techniques enabling them to produce unique and particularly

3

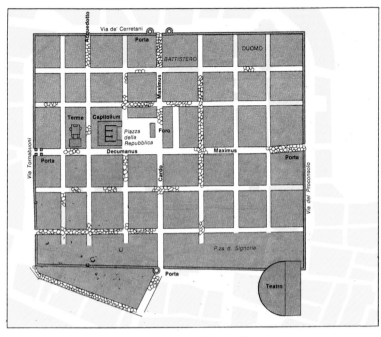

Plan of Roman Florence, overlying today's street-map.

sought-after cloths and colours. In 1252, the town minted its first florin (fiorino), with a fleur-de-lys on one side and the figure of St. John the Baptist on the other; the coin was of solid gold (24 carats) and accepted all over the known world. The strength of this currency, plus the great prosperity of the trading and banking firms and the wool and silk industries, led to the great building boom of the 13th and 14th centuries. The Cathedral of Santa Maria del Fiore, the Belltower, Palazzo della Signoria, the Loggia della Signoria, Santa Croce, the Bargello palace, Santa Maria Novella, Orsanmichele as well as the third circle of walls (1285) were all commenced around this time — despite internecine strife between the pro-emperor Ghibelline and the pro-pope Guelph political factions, wars with the rival cities of Pistoia, Arezzo, Volterra and Siena, and constant plague epidemics, culminating in the terrible Black Death epidemic of 1348, which carried off three-fifths of the population of Europe. It was the age of the guilds, of Dante, Boccaccio and Giotto. So great was the opulence of the city that Pope Boniface VIII's definition of the world entailed five elements: "Earth, Air, Water, Fire and Florentines". In the 14th century, the Alberti and Albizi families rose to power and in the 15th century the wealthy Medici family, backed by the common people, started to gain ever greater political influence. In practice, their status was equivalent to that of a Signoria (Lords of the Town), despite the fact that Florence never ceased to define itself a republic. Cosimo the Elder, founder of the Medici power, was succeeded by his son, Piero the Gouty and by his grandson, the "Magnificent" Lorenzo, a clever politician and an equally clever businessman. The century culminating in Lorenzo's rule, was one of the most splendid in the history of Florence, both in the fields of culture in general, as well as of the arts in particular. It was the age of Humanism and the Renaissance, when the world of the ancient Greeks and Romans was re-discovered and devotedly re-studied. It was in the Renaissance that man claimed for himself the lordship over the whole of Creation, as emanation of the Creator himself. The empirical, dogmatic way of teaching was gradually abandoned in favour of a new scientific method of research. The Renaissance first emerged with Alberti, Brunelleschi, Botticelli and Savonarola. These great innovators were followed by giants like Michelangelo, Leonardo da Vinci, Machiavelli, Galileo and a host of others. It was thanks to their genius that Florence

4

Above: **Roman sarcophagus in the courtyard of the Cathedral Museum**; *below*: **recent excavations in Piazza della Signoria.**

was dubbed the "*Athens of Italy*". For a few more years, between the end of the 15th and the beginning of the 16th century, after Lorenzo's son, the arrogant Piero, had been driven out of Florence, the republican regime was reinstated, but the Medici family returned and Florence was once more subjected to their rule, until 1527, when a new uprising restored the republic, but supported by the Spanish Emperor and the Pope, the Medici family forced its way back on the heels of a fierce siege (1530). In 1569, Cosimo de' Medici, lord of Florence, was granted the title of Grand Duke, a title which was inherited by his successors, until the dynasty died out in 1743, with the death of Anna Maria Ludovica, Princess Palatine. The European powers decreed that the Hapsburgh-Lorraine family should inherit the grandduchy. In 1799 Napoleon installed his family in Tuscany, interrupting the rule of the Hapsburgh-Lorraine dynasty, but in 1814 the Austrian family returned and stayed until Florence and Tuscany were annexed to the newly unified state of Italy (1859). From 1865 to 1871, until Rome was taken from the Popes, Florence was proclaimed capital of Italy. Now Florence is the capital of the Italian region of Tuscany.

FIRST ITINERARY

Piazza del Duomo (Baptistry of San Giovanni; Giotto's Belltower; Loggia del Bigallo; Cathedral of Santa Maria del Fiore; Cathedral Museum) – Medici-Riccardi Palace (Medici Museum) – Piazza San Lorenzo (Church of San Lorenzo, Laurentian Library, Medici Chapels).

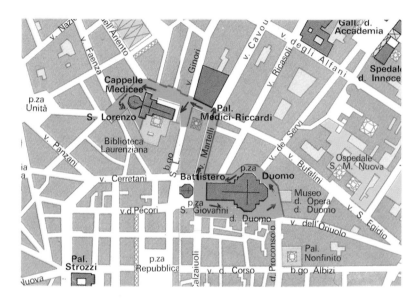

PIAZZA DEL DUOMO

The site of the Piazza, in Roman times, was a mass of houses and public buildings. The church of Santa Reparata was built above the foundations of one of the latter in the 4th century. Three centuries later (though some think in the same century) the Baptistry was built next to the church, and this area began to be the centre of religious life in Florence. Santa Reparata became a cathedral in 1128. The church was becoming too small for its new role and increased importance – the population was increasing too – and in 1289 the Commune decided to enlarge it. This was part of an extensive rebuilding project, involving new and more extensive city walls (the Roman circle was too small), the construction of a Priors' Palace (now Palazzo Vecchio) and alterations to existing buildings such as Santa Croce, the church of the Badia, Orsanmichele, the

6

Bird's eye-view of the Cathedral of Santa Maria del Fiore.

Bargello and the Baptistry. In order to achieve a new, but harmoniously designed city, one man, Arnolfo di Cambio, was given the responsibility of directing and coordinating the work. One of the greatest architects and sculptors of his time, he raised the level of the piazza (which he had re-paved), eliminating the podium on which the Baptistry had previously stood, demolished a few houses nearby, and began to build the new cathedral, for which he planned a dome and external decoration matching that of the Baptistry. The death of Arnolfo in 1302 put a stop to the work, which was resumed in 1332-34 with the construction of the belltower under the direction of Giotto. The addition of a dome by Brunelleschi (1420-36) made it the impressive, dominating building that we see today.

7

Baptistery of St. John — Exterior.

BAPTISTRY

It was described as "*il mio bel San Giovanni*" ("my lovely San Giovanni") by Dante who was christened here in 1265. The baptistery was thought to date back to the 5th century A.D., but is now generally thought to have been built in the Romanesque period (11th-12th centuries) above the site of an Early Christian structure (the foundations of which contain remains of an even earlier, Roman, construction). The exterior of the octagonal building is covered with a typically Romanesque green and white inlaid marble facing. The covering of the dome is concealed behind a 13th century upper storey. The Baptistry was dedicated to St. John the Baptist and served as Florence's cathedral until the year 1128. The three doors, renowned as masterpieces in their own right were restored immediately after the war, but were seriously damaged by the terrible flood of the 4th November 1966. The Eastern, so-called "Paradise" door which was most exposed to the violence of the swirling flood-waters, had five of its panels torn away and is still being restored. Two of the restored

Baptistery — The North Door, by Lorenzo Ghiberti.

panels are in the Museo dell'Opera del Duomo.

THE NORTHERN DOOR — This fine door, often ignored by visitors who would never think of missing Ghiberti's more famous Eastern Door, is also by Ghiberti, who was helped by Donatello, Paolo Uccello, Bernardo Ciuffagni, and Bernardo Cennini. The story of how the door came into being is fascinating. In 1402 a competition for its design was announced, the theme selected being the Sacrifice of Isaac. Some of the most famous artists of the day submitted competition pieces — Ghiberti, Brunelleschi, Jacopo della Quercia, Nicolò Lamberti and many others. The Cathedral Committee judged the bas-reliefs submitted by Brunelleschi and Ghiberti as the two best—but finally awarded the commission to Ghiberti. The committee preferred Ghiberti's elegant composition and refined technique to Brunelleschi's more dramatic but less polished rendition. Modern judges might think differently—in any case, both models are exhibited in the Bargello where everyone may make up his or her own mind. The portal is divided into twenty-eight panels like the south door. The upper twenty illustrate New Testament scenes, the lower eight contain representations of the four Evangelists and Fathers of the Church. Ghiberti's style here is a mixture of Renaissance grace with naturalistic overtones and Gothic sinuousity. The panels show: 1. *St. Ambrose.* — 2. *St. Jerome.* — 3. *St. Gregory.* — 4. *St. Augustine.* — 5. *St. John the Evangelist.* — 6. *St. Matthew.* — 7. *St. Luke.* — 8. *St. Mark.* — 9. *Annunciation.* — 10. *Birth of Jesus.* — 11. *Adoration of the Magi.* — 12. *Jesus debating with the Doctors.* — 13. *Baptism of the Christ.* — 14. *Satan tempts Jesus.* — 15. *Jesus expells the merchants from the Temple.* — 16. *The Apostles are shipwrecked.* — 17. *Christ's transfiguration on Mt. Tabor.* — 18. *Resurrection of Lazarus.* 19. — *Jesus enters Jerusalem.* — 20. *Last Supper.* — 21. *Jesus in the Garden of Gethsemane.* — 22. *Jesus is captured and bound.* — 23. *Jesus is*

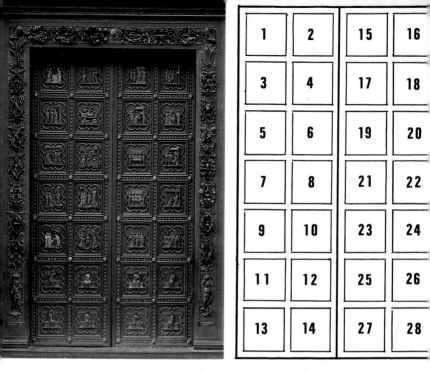

Baptistery — The South Door, by Andrea Pisano.

flogged. — 24. *Pilate washes his hands.* — 25. *Jesus on his way to Calvary.* — 26. *The Crucifixion.* — 27. *The Resurrection.* — 28. *The Descent of the Holy Ghost.* Vittorio Ghiberti cast the foliage, floral, and animal motifs framing the door. The three statues above, by G. Francesco Rustici (1506-1511), represent *Christ between the Levite and the Pharisee.*

THE SOUTH DOOR — This door, created between 1330 and 1336 by Andrea Pisano, is the oldest of the three. It was cast by a Venetian, Leonardo D'Avanzo. The twenty-eight panels illustrate *Scenes from the Life of John the Baptist* and *Allegorical figures* representing the *Cardinal and Theological Virtues.* The episodes illustrated on the panels are: 1. *Zacharias is told of his son's forthcoming birth by the Archangel.* — 2. *Zacharias loses his power of speech.* — 3. *Visitation of Mary to St. Elizabeth.* — 4. *Birth of St. John the Baptist.* — 5. *Zacharias writes John's name on a tablet.* — 6. *St. John withdraws into the desert.* — 7. *St. John preaching to the Pharisees.* — 8. *St. John preaching to the people and the disciples.* — 9. *St. John baptising in the waters of the Jordan.* — 10. *St. John baptizes the Christ.* — 11. *Hope.* — 12. *Faith.* — 13. *Fortitude.* — 14. *Temperance.* — 15. *St. John castigating Herod.* — 16. *St. John is imprisoned.* — 17. *St. John is interrogated by the Jews.* — 18. *St. John announces the advent of the Christ.* — 19. *Salome, Herodias' daughter demands John's head from Herod.* — 20. *St. John is beheaded.* — 21. *Herod banquets while St. John's head is presented to him.* — 22. *Salome presents St. John's head to her mother Herodias.* — 23. *The disciples reverently reclaim St. John's head.* — 24. *The disciples bury the remains of St. John.* — 25. *Charity.* — 26. *Humility.* — 27. *Justice.* — 28. *Prudence.* The frame around the door was designed and cast by Vittorio Ghiberti, son of Lorenzo Ghiberti, in 1462. The bronze statues above the door of the *Baptist, Salome* and the *Executioner beheading the Baptist* are by Vincenzo Danti.

THE EASTERN OR **"PARADISE" DOOR** — Michelangelo defined the eastern
door of the Baptistry as worthy of being the "gates of paradise." Cast in gilded
bronze, the door is the masterpiece of Lorenzo Ghiberti who was 47 when he
undertook the project in 1425 and 74 when he finished it in 1452. Scores of
famous artists of the times were influenced by it: among these we may cite
Michelozzo, Benozzo Gozzoli, Paolo Uccello, Antonio del Pollaiolo, Botticelli,
Domenico del Ghirlandaio, and Michelangelo himself. In the ten panels, which
illustrate Old Testament stories, Ghiberti's use of perspective differs from that of
the Greek and Roman tradition, in which high and low relief figures are used
together, but only along a single plane. Ghiberti instead places his figures,
architecture, animals, and landscape on different planes, thus creating the effect
of a painting in bronze. The enchanting frame with its elaborate decoration
consisting of fruit, flower, animal, and bird motifs, is by the artist's adopted son
Vittorio. The coat of arms of the Merchant Guild which financed the work is
visible at the top. The Wool Merchants ordered that Ghiberti "should do
whatsoever he desired and designed so that the door should be the most
decorated, richest, most perfect and most beautiful imaginable; neither time nor
expense were to be of any consideration, as long as it resulted the finest and most
magnificent of his life's works." On the door frames Ghiberti alternated 24 statues
of prophets and Sibyls with 24 medallions of busts of artists, his contemporaries.

LEFT SIDE — Above, the reclining figure represents *Spring*. From top to bottom,
on the left: the *prophet Amos*, the *prophet Zechariah*, the *prophet Daniel*; *Judith,
daughter of Jephtha*. From top to bottom, right: the *prophet Baruch*, the *prophet
Elijah*, the *Delphic Sibyl*, the *prophet Isaiah*, the *prophet Haggai*. The reclining
figure at the bottom represents *Summer*.

RIGHT SIDE — Above, the reclining figure represents *Autumn*. From top to
bottom, left, the *Tiberine Sibyl*, the *Persian Sibyl*, the *prophet Elisha*, *Joshua*, *the
Cuman Sibyl*. From top to bottom, right: *Judas Maccabeus*, *Samson*, *Jeremiah*,
Gideon, the *prophet Ezekiel*. At the bottom, the reclining figure represents *Winter*.

Creation of Adam and Eve. – Original Sin. – Expulsion from Paradise.

Adam and Eve, Cain and Abel. – Abel keeping sheep and Cain ploughing.– Cain kills Abel. – Curse of Cain.

Story of Noah. – Noah's family leaves the ark after the Flood. – Noah gives thanks to the Lord who sends a rainbow as a sign of peace.– Drunkenness of Noah.– Noah is derided by Ham and covered up by Shem and Japhet.

Story of Abraham: Sarah at the entrance to the tent. – Apparition of the angels to Abraham.– Abraham and Isaac on the mountain.– The Angel stays Abraham's hand as he is about to sacrifice Isaac.

Story of Jacob and Esau: Esau trades his birthright for a plate of lentils.– Isaac sends Esau hunting.– Jacob throws a goat's skin around his neck.– Isaac mistakes Jacob for Esau and gives him his blessing.– Jacob leaves his father's house.

Story of Joseph: Joseph is sold to the merchants and brought before Pharaoh.– Interpretation of Pharaoh's dream. – The golden cup in Benjamin's bag.– Joseph reveals himself to his brothers and forgives them. – Joseph meet Jacob.

Lorenzo Ghiberti

Vittorio Ghiberti

Story of Moses: Moses receives the Tablets of the Law on Mounth Sinai.– Aaron waits halfway down the mountain.– The Hebrews, terrified by the thuder and lightning, await Moses' return at the foot of the mountain.

Story of Joshua: Joshua and the Hebrews cross the Jordan and crowd before the Ark. – The Hebrews gather twelve stones for commemoration.– The walls of Jericho fall at the sound of the Angels' trumpets.

Story of Saul and David: Saul defeats the Philistines.– David smites Goliath.– David carries Goliath's head before the cheering crowd, back to Jerusalem.

King Solomon ceremoniously receives the Queen of Sheba in the Temple of Jerusalem.

Baptistery - The Door of Paradise, by Lorenzo Ghiberti

13

Baptistery — *Above*: **Lorenzo and Vittorio Ghiberti**; *below*: **Zacharias, Elijah, Joshua and Gideon** (details from the Door of Paradise).

The head in the middle of the door between the Delphic Sibyl and the prophet Isaiah is a *self-portrait of Lorenzo Ghiberti*. The one between the prophets Elisha and Joshua is a *portrait* of Bartoluccio (Ghiberti's step-father and teacher), or as some say, of Vittorio, his son. The beautifully decorated door-frame, with its realistically depicted flowers, animals, birds and fruit was cast by Vittorio Ghiberti. On the architrave a statue group of the *Baptism of Christ* by Andrea Sansovino (1502). The *Angel* is by Innocenzo Spinazzi. The group is now being restored. On either side of the door are red porphyry columns. They were captured from the Saracens by the Pisans who then donated them to the Florentines as a token of their gratitude for the Florentines' protection of their city while the Pisan fleet was engaged in the Battle of the Balearic Islands (1117).

Baptistery — Interior.

THE INTERIOR — The eight-sided building has two levels, the lower one with Corinthian columns, the upper one with a narrow arched gallery. The walls are adorned with a geometric multicoloured marble facing which is typical of the Florentine Romanesque style. The inlaid marble pavement of 1209 has zodiacal signs, and motifs which recall Oriental textiles. To the right of the South Door is a marble baptismal font with six bas-relief panels (Pisan school, 1371). Left of the altar is a famous Renaissance wall tomb by Donatello and Michelozzo (1427). It contains the remains of the Antipope John XXIII who died in Florence in 1419. The arch of the apse and dome are aglow with 13th century Byzantine-style mosaics created by mastercraftsmen from Venice and Florence. The mosaics on the vault above the altar were begun in 1225 by Jacopo da Torrita. Their subjects are: *Christ, Mary, Apostles, and Prophets*, and in the double archway, the *Mystic Lamb with Patriarchs and Prophets*. In the center of the ceiling are the *Virgin and Child* on the right, and *John the Baptist enthroned*, on the left. The marble candlestick holder in the shape of an angel to the left of the gallery is by Agostino di Jacopo (1320). The dome mosaics were made by Venetian and Florentine

15

Baptistery — Interior of the dome with its splendid mosaics.

artists in the second half of the 13th and the beginning of the 14th centuries — Cimabue, Andrea di Riccio, known as Tafo, and Gaddo Gaddi. On three sides is a **Last Judgment** with a huge figure of *Christ* (over 26 feet tall). From top to bottom, the subjects in the registers are ornamental motifs, the *heavenly hierarchy*, the *story of the Genesis*, the *story of Joseph*, the *story of Christ*, and the *story of John the Baptist*.

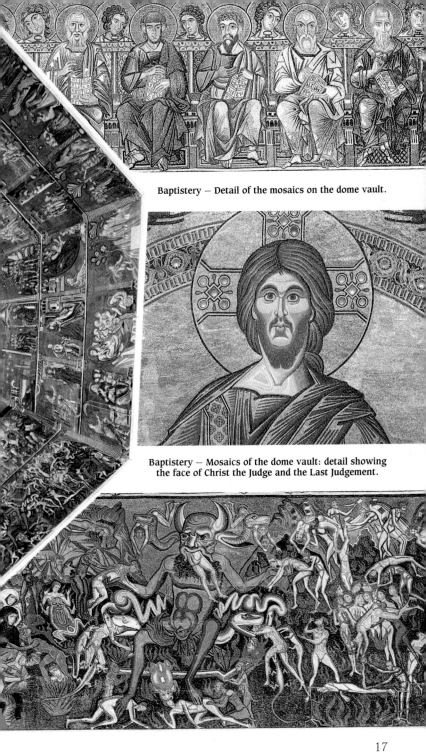

Baptistery — Detail of the mosaics on the dome vault.

Baptistery — Mosaics of the dome vault: detail showing the face of Christ the Judge and the Last Judgement.

Giotto's Belltower.

GIOTTO'S BELL TOWER

The building of this tower began in 1334 under the direction of Giotto, after a fire had destroyed the old bell-tower of Santa Reparata. Giotto died in 1337, when the base of the tower had been completed; work was thereafter directed by Andrea Pisano and Francesco Talenti, who brought it to conclusion (although the original plan included a spire which was never built). The building is of remarkable grace and elegance; the structure lightens and lengthens as it rises, becoming complex with marble insets and fine perforation. The bas-reliefs on the base (the originals are in the Cathedral Museum) were carved by Andrea Pisano and his workmen under the supervision of Giotto. The tower is 84 metres high and one can enjoy a magnificent view from the Terrace (one has to climb 414 steps, to get to the top).

Next to the bell tower, on the corner of Via Calzaioli, the graceful **Loggia del Bigallo**, built between 1352 and 1358 by Alberto Arnoldi, in elegant Gothic style, as a shelter for the town's waifs and orphans (Innocents). Its façade, facing the Baptistry, has three tabernacles with the statues of *St. Peter the Martyr*, the *Virgin and Child* and *St. Luke*. Inside is a fine collection of works of art, with frescoes detached from the building and works by Ghirlandaio, Arnoldi and the schools of Botticelli and Verrocchio. One of the most interesting items is the frescoed *Madonna of Mercy*, with a view of 14th cent. Florence.

Bird's eye-view of the Loggia del Bigallo.

CATHEDRAL

The cathedral was designed in 1296 by Arnolfo di Cambio, who was charged by the Florentine Republic to build it on the site of the pre-existing 4th century church of Santa Reparata, the foundations of which have recently come to light during the excavations carried out after the 1966 flood. The cathedral, financed by the Florentine State, was the most magnificent expression of Medieval faith, power and civic pride in Italy. The 13th century in effect saw the rise of St. Francis and St. Dominic (Faith), the overpowering economical development of the town (Power) and an insurgence of rivalry among the Italian States, to whom Florence wanted to demonstrate that it possessed the most magnificent cathedral (Civic Pride). After the death of Arnolfo (c. 1302), work was interrupted and resumed in 1334, by Giotto, who designed the belltower. When the latter died, in 1337, work again slowed down and it was only between 1357 and 1364 that the Cathedral Overseers entrusted Lapo

Ghini and Francesco Talenti with an even more imposing project than Arnolfo's. In 1378, the vault of the central nave was completed and from 1380 to 1421 the construction of the choir and of the drum of the dome took place. In 1418 a competition was held for the construction of the dome, which was won by Filippo Brunelleschi, who was to devote over fourteen years to the actual building of this magnificent architectural feat which still arouses world-wide admiration. The construction of the cathedral was to take 173 years, due to the continual wars, civil strife, and plagues. After St. Peter in the Vatican and St. Paul's in London, the Florentine cathedral, dedicated to Santa Maria del Fiore is the third longest church in the world (148 metres). It was consecrated by Pope Eugene IV in 1436. The religious rites officiated in the great building before the people of Florence were not the only events that took place there. Among the numerous historical events which took place inside the cathedral, let us recall: the Pazzi Plot (26th April 1478), when Julian de' Medici was assassinated; the last meeting of the Council for the unification of the Greek and Roman Churches (6th July 1436); the fiery sermons of the Dominican Gerolamo Savonarola (1497-98).

Cathedral — Madonna and Child with statues of the Apostles (detail of the façade)

THE FAÇADE — A 19th century Florentine architect, Emilio De Fabris, designed the façade trying to recapture the Florentine Gothic style. The project, which De Fabris worked on until 1871, was continued by Luigi Del Moro who completed it in 1887. The façade is divided into three sections, each of which is topped by a rose window. In the thirteen tabernacles above the doorways are statues of the *Apostles*, the central position being occupied by a *Virgin and Child*, by Tito Sarrocchi. In the four lower tabernacles (from left to right): a *statue of Bishop Valeriani* who blessed the Cathedral's first stone, *Bishop Tinacci* who blessed the first pillar, *Pope Eugene IV* who consecrated the church, and *St. Antoninus* who blessed the façade. The left portal is by Passaglia (1897). The partitions are sculptured with scenes of the life of the Virgin (the *Presentation of Mary at the Temple*, the *Espousal of the Virgin*) and allegorical figures representing the Virtues of *Temperance, Faith, Humility,* and *Prudence*. In the lunette is an allegorical

Cathedral with Giotto's Belltower.

mosaic showing *Charity enthroned*. The central doorway, also by Passaglia (1903), is decorated with the *Conception and the Coronation of the Virgin*, and, in the lunette, *Christ, the Virgin and the patrons of the city*, by Barabino. In the last gable is the *Virgin in Glory* by Passaglia. The scenes depicted on the right door (by Giuseppe Cassioli 1899), are the *Expulsion from Eden*, the *Assumption*, the *Rest on the flight to Egypt*, the *Visitation*, the *Birth of the Virgin*, and the *Annunciation*. Above is a mosaic symbolizing *Faith* based upon cartoons by Barabino.

Cathedral — The Door of the Canons and detail from it showing the Ten Commandments.

SIDES, TRASEPT AND APSE CHAPELS — Starting from the belltower side, a medieval inscription recalls the foundation of the church in 1298; further on, a bas-relief *Annunciation* which used to be in the Oratory of the "Laudese" monks which was demolished to make room for the great belltower. Next comes the **Belltower Door**, of Pisan School. The side pinnacles are surmounted by an *Archangel Gabriel* and a *Virgin*; the tympanum bears the figure of *Jesus blessing*; in the lunette: a delicate *Madonna and Child*. After the fourth twin mullioned window, a pillar marks the end of the early cathedral designed by Arnolfo and the beginning of the part designed by Talenti. The taller, wider-spaced windows lend the whole a majestic, elegant effect. Next comes the **Canons' Door**, which was

Cathedral — View of the apse.

built between 1397 and 1406 by Lorenzo di Giovanni d'Ambrogio, who was responsible for the *Madonna and Child with two Angels* in the lunette; Piero di Giovanni Tedesco and Niccolò d'Arezzo worked jointly on the magnificent door-jambs. From the south-eastern side of the square, one's glance captures the imposing apse of the church. Brunelleschi's splendid octagonal **dome** rears above the three apse chapels and the drum, pierced by wide rose-windows. Beyond the apse, on the left side of the church, one finds the *Almond Door* (**Porta della Mandorla**) which derives its name from the almond-shaped frame surrounding the central sculpted group. It was the last and most beautiful of the doors of the cathedral to be made and the style is a blend of late Gothic and early

Cathedral — One of the apse semi-domes.

Cathedral — **The northern side of the dome from the terrace above the façade
and the Almond Door** (Porta della Mandorla).

Renaissance. The delightful *Madonna of the Girdle* supported by Angels, in the tympanum, is by Nanni di Banco, (1412-1421), who was so worthily succeeded by the great Donatello. The statuettes of the *Prophets*, on the side-pinnacles, were carved by Donatello, between 1405 and 1407, when he was in his twenties. The mosaic in the lunette is by Domenico Ghirlandaio (1491), the *statue of St. Stephen* surmounting the door is by Ciuffagni (1420). The last door towards the façade, called the **Door of the "Balla"** is flanked by two twining columns supported on the right by a lion and on the left by a lioness.

Cathedral — Interior.

THE INTERIOR — The Florentines wanted their cathedral to be sober and austere, yet huge in size so the people of the city could assemble inside. In the shape of a Latin cross, the church has two wide side-aisles separated from the nave by enormous pillars supporting great ribbed vaults. The result is a masterpiece of Florentine Gothic architectural design. The church is 488 feet long, 148 feet wide and 299 feet at the crossing. Inner façade — The stained glass windows above the three western doorways were made from designs by Lorenzo Ghiberti. The mosaic in the lunette above the central door depicting the *Coronation of the Virgin* has been attributed to the 14th century artist Gaddo Gaddi. On either side are frescoes of *Music-making angels* by Santi di Tito (late 16th century). To the right of the door is the *tomb of Antonio d'Orso, Bishop of Florence* (d. 1321), by the Sienese sculptor, Tino di Camaino (14th century). Above is a clock with four heads of prophets painted on the dial by Paolo Uccello (1443). Right aisle — a medallion with a *bust of Brunelleschi* sculpted by a pupil of the great artist, Andrea Cavalcanti, known as Buggiano (1447). Further on is a tabernacle, actually wood but made to resemble marble, with a *statue of Isaiah* attributed to Nanni di Banco

Cathedral — *Left*: Niccolò da Tolentino, by Andrea del Castagno; *right*: John Hawkwood, by Paolo Uccello; *below*: Gothic holy water stoup and St. Zenobius, by Giovanni del Biondo.

Cathedral — Dante and the Divine Comedy, by Domenico di Michelino.

(1408). The medallion just beyond has a *bust of Giotto* by Benedetto da Maiano (1490). The inscription is by the famous scholar Poliziano. A 16th century panel painting of *St. Anthoninus* by Poppi is on the first pier, whereas the Gothic *holy water stoup* is dated around 1380. In the third bay are two false tomb monuments painted by Bicci di Lorenzo in the 15th century. A *bust of Marsilio Ficino* by Andrea Ferrucci (1521) decorates the medallion of the fourth bay. We enter the huge octagonal choir wholly dominated by Brunelleschi's extraordinary dome. The impressive structure rises 296 feet above ground level and measures 149 feet across. The inside of the dome is covered with an enormous *Last Judgment* scene frescoed by Giorgio Vasari and Federico Zuccari (1572-1579). The circular stained glass windows around the eight-sided drum were made from designs by Ghiberti, Donatello, Paolo Uccello and Andrea del Castagno. In the niches of the columns sustaining the dome are eight statues of Apostles, two of which are especially noteworthy (Benedetto da Rovezzano's *St. John*, last column on the right, and Jacopo Sansovino's *St. James the Greater*, left column on the nave side). In the middle is a carved marble choir balustrade designed by Giuliano di Baccio d'Agnolo, but sculpted in 1555 by Baccio Bandinelli who, together with Giovanni Bandini, was also responsible for the bas-reliefs around the choir. The *crucifix* on the main altar is by Benedetto da Maiano (1497). Radiating from the choir is the apse in the middle and a transept on either side, all of which are devided into five small chapels. Between the right transept and the apse is the entrance to the **Old Sacristy** with a glazed terracotta *Ascension* scene by Luca della Robbia (1450) overhead. Standing in the main apse chapel is a bronze urn containing relics of *St. Zenobius*, an outstanding example of Lorenzo Ghiberti's

27

Cathedral — The interior of the dome.

great artistry (1432-1442). The bas-reliefs on the front represent scenes from the life of the saint. Between the apse and the left transept is the so-called **New Sacristy** or, more properly, *"Sagrestia delle Messe"* (Mass Sacristy). Here on April 26, 1478 Lorenzo the Magnificent took refuge during the attempt on his life known in history as the Pazzi Conspiracy (his brother Giuliano, not so fortunate, failed to reach safety and was murdered). The glazed terracotta *Resurrection* above the door, dated 1449, was Luca della Robbia's first experiment in ceramic sculpture. The bronze door is a joint effort by della Robbia, Michelozzo, and Maso di Bartolomeo. Inside is a fine basin by Buggiano (1440) with an angel's head attributed to Mino da Fiesole. The inlaid cupboards are by Giuliano da Maiano (1465). Left aisle: in the fourth bay hangs a well-known painting by Michelino (1465) showing *Dante holding his Divine Comedy*. You see Florence on the left, hell on the right, purgatory in the background, and paradise above. Continuing to the third bay we find Paolo Uccello's famous fresco (transferred onto cloth) of the English soldier of fortune, *Sir John Hawkwood* (1436) and, a bit further on, Andrea del Castagno's equally famous *Captain Niccolò da Tolentino* (also transferred onto cloth) painted just twenty years later. There is also a noteworthy

Cathedral — The Choir; *below*: detail of the relief panels on the Choir enclosure, by Jacopo Sansovino and others.

Cathedral — Resurrection, by Luca della Robbia, above the door of the New Sacristy; *below:* two panels from the door of the New Sacristy.

bust of Antonio Squarcialupi, the organist, by Benedetto da Maiano (1490). The statue of the *Prophet Joshua* in the wooden tabernacle of the first bay supposedly represents Poggio Bracciolini, the famous humanist. It has been attributed to Ciuffagni, Nanni di Bartolo, and Donatello. Off the nave, to the right, steps lead down into the crypt of the church of **Santa Reparata**. These fascinating relics of the past came to light after the 1966 flood and were painstakingly restored.

Cathedral — *Above and below*: **Tomb slabs in Santa Reparata.**

Cathedral — *Above and below, left*: Lamentation over the dead Christ and detail of St. John the Evangelist, 14th century fresco from Santa Reparata; *below, right*: St. Reparata, copy from the original by Arnolfo di Cambio.

The south-eastern side of Piazza del Duomo.

Cathedral Museum — Entrance and bust of Cosimo Ist de' Medici above the entrance.

THE CATHEDRAL MUSEUM

Situated behind the apse of the Cathedral, this museum is of major interest to lovers of fine sculpture. It was opened in 1981 and includes noteworthy masterpieces originally in the Cathedral, in the Belltower or in the Baptistry.

A *bust of Brunelleschi*, two della Robbia *terracotta* and marble *bas-reliefs* by Baccio Bandinelli are displayed in the vestibule. In the first room to our right we

Museum of the Cathedral — The largest room on the ground floor with the statue of Boniface VIII and a Madonna and Child, both by Arnolfo di Cambio.

find fragments of the baptismal font which originally stood in the Baptistry. From here we enter the second room which contains the 15th century statues that once decorated the façade of the Cathedral. Donatello's *St. John*, Nanni di Banco's *St. Luke*, and Bernardo Ciuffagni's *St. Matthew* are outstanding. At the far end of the room is a seated statue of *Pope Boniface VIII*, a 14th century piece from the workshop of the Cathedral's first architect, Arnolfo di Cambio, whereas the *Virgin and Child* nearby was carved by the master himself. The drawing of how Arnolfo's original façade looked (before it was demolished in 1588) is especially interesting. The next room contains illuminated manuscripts, reliquaries, enamels, as well as other valuable pieces from the Cathedral treasury. The painting on the altar at the far end is Bernardo Daddi's *Pregnant Madonna surrounded by saints* (1334). From the second room we enter two newly-opened rooms devoted to Brunelleschi, containing a wooden model of his dome and various technical instruments used in its construction. Retracing our steps through Room 2 we come to the staircase leading to the upper level. On the landing is Michelangelo's renowned **Pietà** (or Deposition). The seventy-eight year-old sculptor used a great marble capital that came from an ancient Roman temple for this group, which he hoped to use as his own grave monument in a chapel he had acquired in Santa Maria Maggiore in Rome. Above the door leading into the main room upstairs are two frescoes of *heads of Apostles* by Bicci di Lorenzo. This room is called the **Sala delle Cantorie** (Choir Loft Room) after the two carved choir lofts displayed here. Originally placed over the sacristy doors (old and new) in the Cathedral the choir-lofts were taken down in 1688. The one near the entrance, by Luca della Robbia (1431-1438), is composed of ten relief panels separated by a row of

Cathedral Museum – The Pietà or Deposition, by Michelangelo.

Cathedral Museum — Overall view of the Room of the Choir-lofts.

squared double pilasters. The youths singing and playing instruments so gracefully represented here illustrate David's psalm *"Laudate Dominum in sanctis eius."* Opposite is Donatello's choir stall (1433-1438). Here winged cupids joyously dance and cavort behind a row of columns suggesting a loggia. In the same room too are the extraordinary statues by Donatello: **Mary Magdalen**, *Jeremiah, Moses,* and *Habakkuk.* The latter is known as *"lo zuccone"* (the pumpkin-head), due to his baldness. Donatello's strongly realistic style in the statues of the prophets for the bell tower becomes astoundingly and exasperatedly tragic in his unique wooden Mary Magdalen. She is not the traditionally youthful beauty, which we find in most Florentine representations of the Saint, but a repentant old woman, a macabre and horrifying apparition of a being consumed by vice, penance and suffering. The *statues of sibyls and prophets* are by Andrea Pisano. The next room, entered from the right, contains paintings, sculptures, and embroidery. Among the highlights are a *Martyrdom of St. Sebastian,* a 14th century *triptych* by Giovanni del Biondo; a wooden inlay with *St. Zenobius and saints* by Giuliano da Maiano; and *Woman with horn of plenty* by Tino di Camaino. Displayed along the walls are several fine 15th century hangings embroidered with *Scenes from the life of St. John the Baptist.* They are based upon designs by Antonio del Pollaiolo. At the far end of the room is a magnificent embossed silver and enamel altar. The most renowned florentine goldsmiths had a hand in the work during the 114 year period (14th-15th century) needed to complete it: Andrea del Verrocchio sculpted the *Beheading of St. John,* Antonio del Pollaiolo, the *Birth of St. John,* Bernardo Cennini, the *Visitation to St. Elizabeth,* to mention some. The *statue of the Baptist* in the middle of the front panel is by Michelozzo, while the *cross* is by Betto Betti, Milano Dei, and Pollaiolo. Two of the restored panels from the "Paradise Door" of the Baptistry are in the centre of the room.

Cathedral Museum — The Magdalen, by Donatello and the precious silver Crucifix, once on the altar of the Baptistery.

Cathedral Museum — The Art of the Blacksmith and the Drunkenness of Noah: two of the marble panels from Giotto's Belltower.

We cross the room with the choir lofts to enter the room containing the original *reliefs of the Labours of Man, the Liberal Arts, the Holy Sacraments, and the Planets*, removed from the belltower. These panels were carved to designs by Giotto, Andrea Pisano, Luca della Robbia, etc.

We turn right as we leave the museum and return to the Cathedral façade. At the corner we turn right into **Via de' Martelli**. Lined with fine shops and important book stores, this is one of Florence's busiest thoroughfares.

Medici Riccardi Palace — The façade.

PALAZZO MEDICI-RICCARDI

Built for Cosimo the Elder, between 1444 and 1460, by the Florentine architect and sculptor Michelozzo Michelozzi, this was the prototype of all Florentine palaces of the Renaissance. Majestic and elegant, it was filled with works of art commissioned by the Medici: the main branch of the family lived here until 1540. In 1655 the palace was sold to the Riccardi family and is now the seat of the provincial administration and the Prefecture. Exhibitions and other cultural events often take place here. Itwas designed by Michelozzo as a large cube, and must have stood out among the lower buildings round it; but the Riccardi family had it enlarged, adding seven new windows on Via Larga (now Via Cavour). The two principal sides, have pronounced rustication on the ground floor, flatter rustication on the storey above and smooth stones on the third. This motif was to reappear frequently for more than a century, along with the use of twin-arched mullioned windows. There is a fine classical cornice, while the big corner windows (called "kneeling windows" from

Medici Riccardi Palace — The Magi's procession on its way towards Bethlehem, by Benozzo Gozzoli (detail).

the form of the corbels) which replaced a previously existing loggia, are attributed to Michelangelo (c. 1517).

Inside the palace is a fine porticoed **courtyard**, that contains Roman remains and various pieces of sculpture. One of the most important items is the **Chapel** by Michelozzo, at the top of the first staircase on the right from the courtyard. Here are the celebrated frescoes by Benozzo Gozzoli representing the *Journey of the Three Kings to Bethlehem* (1459-60) in which many personages of the time are portrayed: Lorenzo the Magnificent with his father, Piero the Gouty and his sisters; Galeazzo Maria Sforza; Sigismondo Malatesta; John VII Paleologus, Emperor of Constantinople; the painter himself and his master, Fra Angelico. There is also an interesting **Gallery**, reached by going up the second staircase on the right, from the courtyard, decorated with stuccoes and mirrors at the end of the 18th century, with a fine frescoed ceiling by Luca Giordano showing the *Apotheosis of the Medici dynasty* (1682-83).

After leaving the palace, the short Via dei Gori - flanking the building to one's right - leads into **Piazza San Lorenzo** — a picturesque and lively market square, dominated by the cumbersome bulk of the church of San Lorenzo with the Chapel of the Princes' dome behind it. The monument to *Giovanni dalle Bande Nere*, by Baccio Bandinelli (1540) stands at the Via dei Gori corner of the square.

39

San Lorenzo — the façade.

SAN LORENZO

The church, originally on this site, was consecrated in 393 by St. Ambrose, Bishop of Milan. The Romanesque church constructed around the year 1000 which replaced it was redesigned between 1421 and 1446 by Brunelleschi who had received the commission from Giovanni Bicci de' Medici, although the project was not finished until 1460 by Brunelleschi's pupil, Antonio Manetti. Michelangelo too, commissioned by his Medici patrons, worked on the great church. He designed the façade which, however, was never carried out.

THE INTERIOR — The double row of slender Corinthian columns surmounted by rounded arches rhythmically spaced along the nave and the typically Brunelleschian grey (*pietra serena*) and white (plaster) colour scheme combine to create an effect of incomparable harmony and elegance. The balcony high up on the inner façade was designed by Michelangelo. The two facing pulpits in the last bays standing in the nave near the altar are the last works of Donatello, who was working on them when he died in 1466. They were finished by his pupils,

San Lorenzo — Central nave; *below*: Martyrdom of St. Laurence, by Agnolo Bronzino (detail).

San Lorenzo — The cloisters with their Brunelleschi lines.

Bertoldo and Bellano. Along the right aisle (second chapel) is Rosso Fiorentino's *Espousal of the Virgin*, a fine 16th century painting, and further on (last bay) is Desiderio da Settignano's carved marble *tabernacle*, a masterpiece of 15th century sculpture. Along the left aisle (last bay) is a fresco by Bronzino, the *Martyrdom of St. Laurence* (1569). At the foot of the steps leading up to the main altar, a bronze grating marks the spot where Cosimo the Elder, called *"Pater Patriae"* (father of his country) is buried. From the far side of the left transept we enter the **Sacrestia Vecchia**, or Old Sacristy. Despite its small size, it ranks as one of Brunelleschi's finest creations, an outstanding example of spatial harmony achieved by combining rhythmic and geometric effects. The painted stucco medallions in the pendentives of the hemispherical dome which illustrate *scenes from the life of John the Baptist* are by Donatello, as are the four *Evangelists* in the lunettes, the *frieze with cherubs*, the two bronze portals on either side of the altar with *Fathers of the Church* and *Apostles* on the panels, and the magnificent terracotta bust of *St. Laurence* on the cabinet. The sarcophagus in the centre, sculptured by Andrea Cavalcanti, *"il Buggiano"*, is the tomb of Giovanni Bicci and Piccarda de' Medici, Cosimo the Elder's parents, while the bronze and prophyry one on the left beneath the archway, a masterpiece by Verrocchio (1472), is the burial place of Cosimo's sons, Giovanni and Piero. Returning to the church proper, we turn right into the 14th century **Martelli Chapel** with a lovely 15th century Filippo Lippi *Annunciation* on the altar and a *tomb monument to Donatello* on the righthand wall which was sculpted in 1896 by Romanelli.

Laurentian Library — The Michelangelo-Ammannati staircase in the vestibule.

THE LAURENTIAN LIBRARY

The library, reached from the square at number 9 (alongside the church) is at the far end of a lovely, 15th century Brunelleschi-style **cloister**, up a flight of stairs. Founded by Cosimo the Elder and later enlarged by Lorenzo the Magnificent, this is one of the world's finest libraries. It was wholly designed by Michelangelo, although the vestibule which Michelangelo started work on in 1524 was completed by Ammannati and other architects.

Its incomparable collections include codices, manuscripts, and illuminated missals dating from the 6th to 15th centuries, Lorenzo the Magnificent's prayerbook, and autographs of famous personages ranging from Petrarch to Napoleon. The reading room, nearly 165 feet long, is lit by 15 stained glass windows designed by Giovanni da Udine. The wooden ceiling, desks, and lecterns were all designed by Michelangelo and carried out by Tribolo and others.

Back in Piazza San Lorenzo, we continue along the right side of the church building and in Piazza Madonna degli Aldobrandini (behind the church) we enter the Medici Chapels.

MEDICI CHAPELS

The shrine and mausoleum of the Medici, by the church of San Lorenzo (the entrance is at the back of the church in Piazza Madonna degli Aldobrandini), the Medici chapels are an important architectural and artistic complex, famous above all for the statues by Michelangelo. The Princes' Chapel is also impressive on the outside: its structure resembles that of the dome of the Cathedral, octagonal in form with a small apse.

Inside, there is first a wide crypt, which leads up to the sumptuous **Princes' Chapel**, ordered by Ferdinando I in 1602. The design is by Giovanni de' Medici, Matteo Nigetti, and Buontalenti, and work continued for more than a century. The great octagonal space is lined with inlaid semi-precious stone wall-panels of spectacular effect. Against the walls are the sarcophagi of six Medici grand dukes; above those of Ferdinando I and Cosimo II, statues in gilt bronze by Ferdinando Tacca; below: the sixteen coats of arms of Tuscan cities, in inlaid semi-precious stones, is a modern reconstruction, with pieces from various periods. The frontal has a representation of the *Supper at Emmaus*. The chapel-dome is frescoed with *Scenes from the Old and New Testament*, by Pietro Benvenuti (1828). A corridor leads to the **New Sacristy**, the famous and beautiful chapel built by Michelangelo for Cardinal Giulio de' Medici, later Pope Clement VII. Michelangelo worked on it, through various vicissitudes, from 1520 until his patron, who had given him a completely free hand, died and he left Florence for good (1534). The chapel was

Medici Chapels — Interior of the Chapel of the Princes; *below*: **The Supper at Emmaus** (detail of the altar frontal).

never finished. On a square plan, it resembles the structure of Brunelleschi's Old Sacristy, but with much richer and more complex architectural decoration (niches, windows, arches, etc.). The only complete tombs are those of two minor members of the great Florentine family; Giuliano, Duke of Nemours, and Lorenzo, Duke of Urbino, son of Piero the Unfortunate. The two tombs, facing each other are placed on either side of the altar, in a splendid architectural setting of white

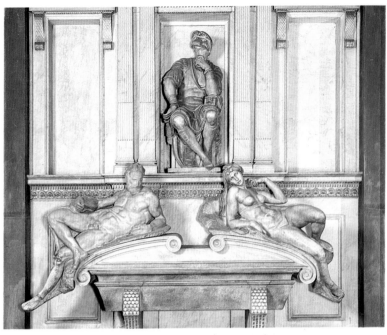

Medici Chapels — The tomb of Lorenzo, duke of Urbino, by Michelangelo (New Sacristy).

marble and grey stand-stone (pietra serena). The idealised figures of the two young men in Roman dress and armour sit above the two sarcophagi. *Giuliano*, Duke of Nemour's tomb is on the right, looking at the altar, with reclining figures of *Night* (a gleaming, polished moon-like female figure sunk in sleep) and *Day* (a relaxed, muscular male figure, whose deliberately unfinished features half-concealed behind his powerful hunched shoulder evoke the sun rising behind a mist-shrouded mountain) at each end of his sarcophagus. *Lorenzo*, duke of Urbino is sunk in thought (he has in fact been nick-named "Pensieroso" - "the Thinker"). The reclining figures on his sarcophagus represent *Dawn* (a newly awakened girl, stretching herself voluptuously) and *Dusk* (a weary old man, whose grey exhaustion seems to have eaten away his fading features). The curving volutes surmounting the two urns symbolically enable the souls of the two dukes to flee the confines of space and time, to attain the trascendental domain of Eternity. Above the sarcophagus containing the remains of Lorenzo the Magnificent and his brother Giuliano, killed in the Pazzi conspiracy, is the beautiful *Virgin and Child*, also by Michelangelo, upon whom both dukes have fixed their gaze; at the sides, *St. Cosmas* (left) by Montorsoli and *St. Damian* (right) by Raffaello da Montelupo, works by two pupils of Michelangelo that fall far below the expressive achievement of the statues near them. This work by Michelangelo, though unfinished, is generally interpreted as a lofty meditation on human destiny, its vanity and its redemption by religious faith. The two zones of the chapel can be understood in this sense: the lower order, with the tombs and allegorical statues, represents all-consuming Time that leads inexorably to death, and its effect on everything in the terrestrial sphere, whilst the upper one, more luminous with the lunettes and the cupola, represents the vault of Heaven and Eternity.

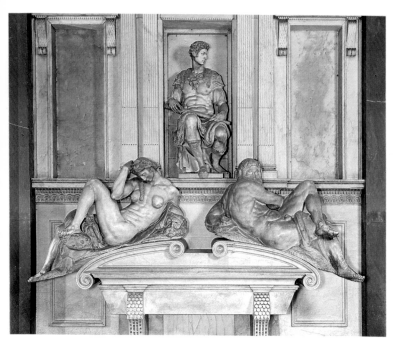

Medici Chapels — The tomb of Julian, duke of Nemours, by Michelangelo;
below: Madonna and Child, by Michelangelo between Saints Cosmas (*left*) and
Damian (*right*), by Montorsoli and Raffaello da Montelupo (New Sacristy).

LORENZO IL MAGNIFICO E GIVLIANO DEI MEDICI

SECOND ITINERARY

Piazza del Duomo – Via Calzaiuoli – Church of Orsanmichele – Piazza della Signoria (Loggia dei Lanzi, Palazzo Vecchio) – Piazzale degli Uffizi (Uffizi Gallery)

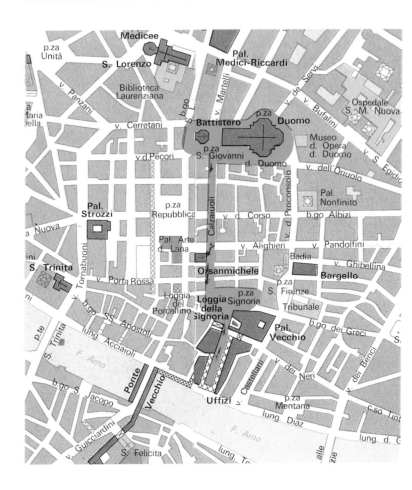

Via de' Calzaiuoli — This shop and boutique-lined thoroughfare connects Piazza della Signoria and Piazza del Duomo. Just off Piazza del Duomo, plaques on buildings indicate the sites of the studios where Donatello and Michelozzo worked. Further on, a few yards beyond Via Tosinghi, Via del Corso intersects Via dei Calzaiuoli and continues as Via degli Speziali on the right. If you turn into Via degli Speziali, you soon come to a bustling 19th century square, called Piazza della Repubblica. If, instead you go straight on towards Piazza della Signoria, you will encounter, on the right side, the church of Orsanmichele.

48

The square bulk of Orsanmichele.

ORSANMICHELE

When Arnolfo di Cambio built it in 1290 he had to tear down the church of San Michele Arcangelo then on the site. Since San Michele was surrounded by a garden (*orto* in Italian) it came to be known as Orto di San Michele, whence Orsanmichele. Arnolfo's open arcade was the *"loggia del grano"* (wheat arcade), where the grain market was. When it was destroyed in a fire in the 14th century, it was rebuilt by the foremost Florentine architects of the day, namely Francesco Talenti, Neri di Fioravante, Benci di Cione, and Simone di Francesco Talenti. Their design included two upper stories above the loggia which would serve as the city's central grain deposit to be used by the citizens during emergencies. The building, was begun in 1337 and fully completed in 1404. In 1349, while building was still under way, it was decided that the open loggia should be turned into an oratory, although not until 1380 did Simone di Francesco Talenti wall in the open arches. He inserted superbly delicate tracery in the upper portion of each walled-up triple-mullioned arch. The statues decorating the niches on all four sides of the building represent the patron saints of the *Arti Maggiori* (Guilds) and were commissioned from the great sculptors of the 14th, 15th, and 16th centuries such as Nanni di Banco, Donatello, Giambologna, and others.

Orsanmichele — Interior.

Starting left of the entrance on Via de' Calzaiuoli: 1) the Wool Merchants Guild shrine with *St. John the Baptist* by Lorenzo Ghiberti (1414-1416); 2) the Tribunal of the Guilds shrine by Donatello and Michelozzo with bronze statues of *Christ and St. Thomas* by Verrocchio (1464-1483) and 3) the Judges' and Notaries' Guild shrine with *St. Luke* by Giambologna (1601). Along Via Orsanmichele side: the Butcher's Guild shrine with *St. Peter* by Donatello (1408); 2) the Tanners' Guild shrine with *St. Philip* by Nanni di Banco (1405-1410); 3) the Builders' and Sculptors' Guild shrine with the *"Quattro Coronati"* (four saints) by Nanni di Banco (1408); 4) the *Armourers' shrine* with a copy of Donatello's *St. George* (the original, dated 1416, has been moved to the Bargello Museum). Along Via della Lana: 1) the Moneychangers' Guild shrine with *St. Laurence* by Lorenzo Ghiberti (1420), the Wool Guild shrine with *St. Stephen* by Lorenzo Ghiberti (1428); 3) the Blacksmiths' Guild shrine with *St. Eligius* by Nanni di Banco (1415). Along Via dei Lamberti: 1) the Linen Merchants Guild shrine with *St. Mark* by Donatello (1411-1413); 2) the Furriers' Guild shrine with a *St. Jacob* and a bas-relief attributed to Ciuffagni; 3) the Physicians' and Pharmacists' Guild shrine with a *Virgin and Child* attributed to Simone Talenti; 4) the Silk Merchants Guild shrine with *St. John the Evangelist* by Baccio da Montelupo (1515).

THE INTERIOR — The simple rectangular space, divided into two parts, is illuminated by glowing stained-glass windows. The ceiling is covered with 14th and 15th century frescoes of the guilds' patron saints. Dominating the interior is Orcagna's huge canopied **tabernacle** of 1349-1359, an impressive masterpiece of the International Gothic style (the influence of this style was being felt in Florence towards the mid 1300s). The relief panels around the base depict *Scenes from the Life of the Virgin*. Starting from the *Birth of the Virgin*, the story continues with the *Presentation of Mary at the Temple*, the *Espousal of the Virgin*, the *Annunciation*, the *Nativity*, the *Presentation of Jesus at the Temple*, the

The Guild Hall of the Wool Merchants.

Annunciation of the Death of the Virgin. The statues on the columns represent *Prophets, Sybils, Virtues*, and *Apostles* with a figure of the *Saviour* on the top of the dome. Of all the reliefs, the finest is the *Assumption of the Virgin* on the back. The clean-shaven hooded man is a self-portrait of the artist. The panel of the *Madonna delle Grazie* on the altar, dated 1352, is by Bernardo Daddi. On the altar to the left of the tabernacle is a marble group, the *Madonna and Child with St. Anne*, by Francesco da Sangallo (1526).

Leaving the church from the main door, we are in front of the **Palazzo dell'Arte della Lana** (the Wool Merchants' Guild) which is linked to the church by a raised passageway. Built in 1300, it was the headquarters of one of Florence's wealthiest guilds. In 1905, it was restored and turned over to the local Dante Society. Inside, traces of 15th century frescoes are still visible. On the corner of the building is a lovely Gothic shrine known as "St. Mary of the Trumpet", containing a 14th century painting of the *Virgin with Angels* and *Saints* and the *Coronation of the Virgin* by Jacopo Landini known as *"il Casentino."*.

Back on Via Calzaiuoli we encounter a charming little church opposite Orsanmichele: **San Carlo dei Lombardi**. Begun in 1349 by Neri di Fioravante and Benci di Cione, it was finished by Simone Talenti in 1384. Inside is a 14th century painting by Niccolò Gerini, a dramatic rendering of the *Burial of Christ*.

Bird's eye-view of Piazza della Signoria.

PIAZZA DELLA SIGNORIA

Via Calzaiuoli ends in Piazza della Signoria. In Roman times, the area that is now the civic centre of the town was occupied by dwellings and an amphitheatre. At the end of the 13th century, the area was included in Arnolfo di Cambio's project: he requisitioned and pulled down the houses of Ghibelline families standing there and began to build Palazzo Vecchio. Henceforward the piazza became the setting for public speeches, ceremonies, meetings, uprisings, executions: in this context one recalls Gerolamo Savonarola, the preacher who was for a short time, the arbiter of political life in the city and was excommunicated and burnt at the stake as a heretic on May 23rd, 1498, on the spot now indicated by a plaque in the paving in front of the Neptune Fountain.

Loggia dei Lanzi or Loggia of the Signoria — Exterior; *below*: the interior with its famous collection of statues.

LOGGIA DEI LANZI

This is also called the Loggia della Signoria because it was built to shelter the public ceremonies of the Signoria (or ruling assembly) or also the Loggia dell'Orcagna from the name of the architect who, according to Vasari, designed it. The Lanzi were the Lanzichenecchi (Landsknechts),

Loggia of the Signoria — Perseus, by Benvenuto Cellini and Rape of the Sabine women, by Giambologna.

German mercenaries in the pay of Cosimo I, who used the Loggia as their bivouac for a certain period. The Loggia was built between 1376 and 1383 by Benci di Cione and Simone Talenti.

It consists of three large classical arches, supported by composite pillars and a spacious cross-vaulted porch. The lobed panels between the arches were carved between 1384 and 1389 upon designs by Agnolo Gaddi and enclose statues of the *Virtues*. Two heraldic *lions* flank the entrance: the one on the right is an ancient Roman statue, the other is 16th century. Beneath the right arch is the **Rape of the Sabines**, by Giambologna (1583), a work of refined virtuosity, which introduces the Baroque and was principally conceived to present and solve novel technical and compositional problems, wherefore it only received its name after it

Piazza della Signoria — The Neptune Fountain, by Bartolommeo Ammannati.

was finished. The left arch frames the **Perseus** by Benvenuto Cellini (1546-54): the hero holding up the head of Medusa has a classical stateliness and an almost Manneristic grace; the base is splendid, with statues and bas-reliefs that reveal the artist's skill as a goldsmith (the original statuettes and panel are now in the Bargello museum and have been replaced by copies). The loggia also contains *Hercules and Nessus*, another group by Giambologna, *Menelaus bearing the body of Patroclus*, a Roman copy of a Greek original of the 4th century B.C.; *six Roman female statues* and the *Abduction of Polixena*, by the nineteenth century sculptor, Pio Fedi.

On the side opposite the Loggia, at N° 5, is the **Alberto della Ragione collection** (works of contemporary Italian art) and at N° 7, **Palazzo Uguccioni**, built to a design by Michelangelo or Raphael, and on the east side the **Tribunal of the Guilds**, built in 1359.

Neptune Fountain — Bartolomeo Ammannati was architect to Grand Duke Cosimo. He designed the courtyard of Pitti Palace, the Carraia and Santa Trinita bridges and worked on numerous mansions all over Florence; as a sculptor, his most important work is this fountain in the piazza, commissioned by Cosimo and sculpted between 1563 and 1576. In the centre of the polygonal pool is the imposing figure of *Neptune* (whose bearded features recall the artist's patron, Cosimo), standing on a coach drawn by sea-horses; all round the edge of the pool the magnificent bronze figures of *Naiads*, *Tritons* and *Satyrs* reveal the hand of Giambologna, Ammannati's assistant. On the steps of the Palace: the *Marzocco*,

55

the lion of the Florentine republic, a copy of Donatello's original, now in the Bargello; Donatello's *Judith and Holophernes*, a bronze copy of the original, now inside Palazzo Vecchio; a copy of Michelangelo's *David*; now in the Academy, placed here in 1504; *Hercules and Cacus* by Bandinelli (1534) and two statuettes (perhaps *Philemon* and *Baucis* changed into plants) by De' Rossi and Bandinelli.

Next to the fountain is an imposing **equestrian monument to Cosimo I de' Medici** by Giambologna (1594). The reliefs around the base represent: *The Tuscan Senate conferring the title of grandduke on Cosimo I* (1537), *Pius V presenting Cosimo with the insignia of the rank of grandduke* (1569), and *Cosimo victoriously entering Siena* (1557).

PALAZZO VECCHIO

The palace was used as the headquarters of the main communal authorities throughout the 14th century and as headquarters of the Medici dukes up to the middle of the 16th century, when Cosimo Ist moved to Palazzo Pitti. Between 1865 and 1871, it housed the Chamber of Deputies of the newly founded Kingdom of Italy. Its austere, imposing appearance is enhanced by the soaring 94 meter tower rising asymmetrically above the façade. According to tradition, it was built by *Arnolfo di Cambio* between 1298 and 1314. The palace consists of a great four-sided building of rusticated stone, with a double tier of lovely Gothic twin-mullioned windows crowned by massive battlements. The slender, rectangular

Palazzo della Signoria — The Michelozzo courtyard.

Tower with its double crown of battlements bears a great staff supporting the lion rampant and the lily, the symbols of Florence, which, in the words of a decree issued by the Lords of the City (Signoria) "be like the cross above a church, attesting that it has been consecrated to God, thus our lion stands for the liberty and strength of the Republic of Florence". At the bottom of the tower is a tiny prison cell called the *Alberghetto*, where Cosimo the Elder and later Gerolamo Savonarola (in the 45 days he was kept imprisoned and tortured before his execution) were kept prisoners. The *clock*, added in the 15th century, was later restored by Vincenzo Galilei and in 1667, by a master clock-maker from Augsburg, named Georg Lederle. The nine coats of arms that decorate the spaces between the brackets below the gallery, beneath the battlements, represent the successive lords and regimes who presided over the Florentine Republic. Above the main entrance there are two lions (placed there in 1528) supporting the *Monogramme of Christ* resting on a tablet bearing the words "Rex Regum et Dominus Dominantium" (King of kings and Lord of lords), placed there first after the first expulsion of the Medici family (1494) and by Cosimo Ist in 1551 to stress the devotion of the Florentines to the Saviour, sole leader of their Republic.

THE INTERIOR — The **courtyard** is a charming introduction to the palace. The harmonious Renaissance-style arcade was designed by Michelozzo in 1453, although the frescoes and stucco decoration on the column were not added until 1565. The courtyard was decorated with frescoed scenes of Austrian and Hungarian towns to celebrate the wedding between Francesco de' Medici and Joanna of Austria. In the centre of the courtyard is a *porphyry fountain* designed

Palazzo della Signoria — *Above*: the Hall of the Five Hundred; *below*: Pisa besieged and overthrown, by Giorgio Vasari (detail).

59

II			A	B	C		IV	
3	10	12	15	18	21	24	27	30	33	40	42
2	9	11								39	41
1	(8)	14	17	20	(23)	26	29	32	(38)		
5	7	13	16	19	22	25	28	31	35	37
4	6								34	36
I	D	E	F	III				

Plan showing the arrangement and the subjects painted on the ceiling of the Hall of the Five Hundred.

by Vasari and crafted by Battista del Tadda in 1557. It is decorated with a charming winged cupid holding a dolphin, a copy of Verrocchio's original of 1476 recently moved upstairs (2nd floor) to preserve it from pollution. In a niche under the portico is a marble group of *Samson and the Philistine* by Pierino da Vinci. At the far left end is the entrance to the **Sala delle Armi** (Armoury), which, unlike most of the palace, retains its original 14th century appearance.

THE FIRST FLOOR — **The Hall of the 500** is of truly imposing proportions: 173 feet long, 71 feet wide, and 58 feet high. Built by Simone del Pollaiolo (called Cronaca) in 1495 after the Medici had been driven out of the city (in 1494) and a republic with Savonarola at its head replaced them, it was used for meetings of the People's Great Assembly, composed of 500 citizens. When the Medici were reinstated, Cosimo I commissioned Baccio d'Agnolo and Baccio Bandinelli to redecorate the hall so it could be used for receptions and public audiences, Later, Giorgio Vasari, a writer as well as a painter and architect, enlarged it and decorated it (1560-1572). In 1503 Pier Soderini, a leading city official, had commissioned Leonardo da Vinci and Michelangelo to decorate a wall each with frescoes commemorating famous Florentine battles. But nothing ever came of the project, except for a preliminary design for the Battle of Anghiari (Leonardo) and one for an episode of the war against Pisa (Michelangelo), the cartoons of which have either been lostor destroyed. The ceiling of the Hall is divided into 39 panels, supported by splendidly carved and gilded frames, painted by Vasari and his helpers with episodes from the *history of Florence and of the Medici family* revolving around the central panel depicting the *apotheosis of Cosimo Ist*. The subjects depicted are as follows: 1. *Cherubs with the Medici spheres.* — 2. *Portraits of the artists who painted the ceiling.* — 3. *Cherubs with a scroll commemorating the hall in Latin.* — Territories belonging to Florence: 4. *Prato.* — 5. *Pistoia.* — 6. *Pescia.* — 7. *Lower Valdarno.* — 8. *The quarters of San Giovanni and Santa Maria Novella.* — 9. *Fiesole.* — 10. *Romagna.* — 11. *Mugello.* — 12. *Casentino.* — 34. *Chianti.* — 35. *Certaldo.* — 36. *San Gimignano.* — 37. *Volterra.* — 38. *Quarters of Santa Croce and Santo Spirito.* — 39. *Upper Valdarno.* — 40.

Palazzo della Signoria — *Left*: **Victory, by Michelangelo;** *right*: **Hercules and Diomedes, by Vincenzo de' Rossi** (Hall of the Five Hundred).

Borgo San Sepolcro. — 41. *Arezzo.* — 42. *Cortona.* — Salient episodes of the Pisan War: 13. *The taking of Cascina.* — 16. *Antonio Giacomini inciting the Florentines to fight.* — 19. *The taking of Vico Pisano.* — 22. *Pisan prisoners at the San Frediano Gate of Florence.* — 25. *The siege of Pisa and the defeat of the French troops.* — 28. *The Venetian defeat at the Verna (1498).* — 31. *Pisan brigs loaded with grain, captured by the Florentine galleys.* — Salient episodes from the War against Siena: 15. *The taking of Monastiro.* — 18. *Cosimo planning the taking of Siena.* — 21. *The taking of Casole.* — 24. *The triumphal reception of the Marquis of Marignano.* — 27. *The taking of Monteriggioni.* — 30. *The Battle of Scannagallo.* — 33. *The Turkish pirates repulsed off the coast of Piombino.* — Origins and development of Florence: 14. *Radagaisus, King of the Goths, defeated by Honorius (407).* — 17. *Octavian, Lepidus and Mark Anthony found Florence.* — 20. *Clement IVth hands the Guelph ensigns to the Florentines.* — 23. *Apotheosis of Cosimo Ist de' Medici.* — 26. *Eugene IVth lands in Leghorn, protected by the Florentines.* — 29. *The building of the third circle of the walls of Florence is begun (1284).* — 32. *The alliance between Florence and Fiesole.* — Painted on slate panels along the top of the walls of the hall: — I *Boniface VIIIth expresses his admiration to the Florentine ambassadors.* — II. *Cosimo Ist receives the insignia of Grand Duke of Tuscany.* — III. *Cosimo Ist is appointed duke of Tuscany by the Florentine Senate.* — IV. *Cosimo Ist founds the knightly order of St. Stephen.* — Frescoes on the walls: — A. *The taking of Siena.* — B. *The capitulation of Porto Ercole.* — C. *The victory of Marciano.* — D. *The assault on Pisa.* — E. *Maximilian tries to conquer Leghorn.* — F. *The Pisans are defeated at*

Palazzo della Signoria – The ceiling of the Hall of the Five Hundred; *below*: Siena taken during the night, by Giorgio Vasari (detail).

Torre San Vincenzo. The subjects of the *Tapestries*, below the frescoes, woven in the Medici tapestry works, are *scenes from the life of St. John the Baptist*. The statues along the walls by Vincenzo de' Rossi represent the *Labours of Hercules*. The door at the far end (generally locked) leads to the **ricetto** (entrance hall) decorated by Lorenzo Sabatini and the **Sala degli Otto di Pratica** with a magnificent carved wooden ceiling by Benedetto da Maiano and Marco del Tasso and 18th century Gobelins tapestries decorating the walls. From the *ricetto* we enter the **Sala dei Duecento** (Hall of the 200). It was named Hall of the 200 because the Council of 200 (citizens) used to meet here at the time of the Republic to debate on major decisions. The hall was designed by Benedetto and Giuliano da Maiano (1472-1477). Giuliano also designed the lovely ceiling decorated with carved fleur-de-lis. The superb *tapestries* on the walls (now being restored), woven in Florence, show *scenes from the life of Joseph*. These rooms are now used by the mayor and the town council. Returning to the Hall of the 500, we turn to the wall to the left of the entrance, which has three huge arched windows beneath it: a platform where the grandduke would sit during public audiences. This section of the hall was aptly known as l'**Udienza** (the Audience). The statues in the niches are, from left to right, *Giovanni delle Bande Nere* by Bandinelli, *Leo X*, by Bandinelli and Vincenzo de' Rossi, and *Alessandro de'*

Palazzo della Signoria — The Studiolo or little Cabinet of Francesco Ist de' Medici.

Medici, by Bandinelli. The marble group by Michelangelo dated 1525 representing the *Victory of Genius over brute force* stands halfway down the wall to one's right facing the dais of the "Udienza". To right, at the other end, to the right of the entrance, is the door leading into the so-called **Studiolo of Francesco I** designed by Vasari (1570-1572) as a place where the scholarly and art loving prince could withdraw from the world. Every square inch is decorated: there are paintings, frescoes, bronze statuettes, as well as stucco decoration and inlays. The ceiling panels are by Francesco Morandini, known as *"il Poppi"*. The slate portraits in the lunette by Bronzino are of Francesco's parents, *Cosimo I and Eleonora of Toledo*. The closet doors are decorated with mythological scenes and historical episodes painted by two famous 16th century Florence Mannerists, Bronzino and Allori. In the eight niches along the upper section of the wall are lovely bronze statuettes such as: Giambologna's *Apollo* (last, right wall) and Ammannati's *Venus* (opposite the Apollo) which are outstanding. From the left side, through a tiny door disguised as a cabinet, we can enter the *Tesoretto*, the secret writing room that Vasari created for Cosimo I.

Palazzo della Signoria – The Clement VIIth Room; *below*: Cosimo the Elder re-enters Florence after his exile, by Giorgio Vasari.

By way of the Hall of the 500, we enter the **Leo X** Apartments (these apartments are not always open to the public as they are part of the mayor's offices). Frescoed with scenes of Medici history by Vasari and his helpers, the rooms are named after famous Medicis: **Sala di Leone X**; **Sala di Clemente VII** (with a famous fresco of Florence during the siege of 1529); **Sala di Giovanni delle Bande Nere**; **Sala di Cosimo il Vecchio, Sala di Lorenzo il Magnifico**, and **Sala di Cosimo I**.

Palazzo della Signoria — Filippo Brunelleschi presents Cosimo the Elder with the model of the Basilica of San Lorenzo, by Giorgio Vasari (Room of Cosimo the Elder).

THE SECOND FLOOR — From the *Sala di Leone X*, we take the stairs to the second floor. To the left, off the top landing, is the entrance to the **Quartiere degli Elementi**, a suite designed by Bernardo del Tasso (1550). The name *"degli elementi"* comes from the frescoes by Vasari and Cristoforo Gherardi (known as *"il Doceno"*) with representations of the elements of *fire, water, earth and air*. From the *Sala degli Elementi* we enter the **Terrazzo di Saturno** which gets its name from the allegory on the ceiling. The *terrazzo* commands a splendid panoramic view of the city surrounded by the hills of Settignano, Piazzale Michelangelo, and Forte Belvedere. From the left we enter the **Sala di Ercole**. The ceiling fresco by Gherardi represents the *Labours of Hercules*. On the wall is a 16th century Florentine tapestry depicting *Hercules slaying the Centaur* after a drawing by Stradano. From the **Sala di Giove** with a ceiling fresco of the *Childhood of Jupiter*, we come back to the *Sala degli Elementi* and from here, taking the door on the right, we enter the **Camera di Berecinzia**, with Florentine allegorical tapestries and the *Triumph of Berecinzia* and the *Four Seasons* on the ceiling by Vasari and Gherardi. Next is the **Sala di Cerere** with a fresco of *Ceres in search of Proserpine* by Gherardi. The tapestries, after cartoons by Stradano, show hunting scenes. A door at the far end leads to the **Writing Room** (or **Sala di Calliope**, from Vasari's ceiling fresco). Here Cosimo I used to work on his

Palazzo della Signoria — Hall of the Elements, *below*: the Jupiter Room.

Palazzo della Signoria – The Audience Hall.

collection of precious *objets d'art* (jewelry, miniatures, and bronzes) now displayed in the Pitti Palace.

Leaving the *Quartiere degli Elementi* on our way to the **Quartiere di Eleonora di Toledo** we cross the Hall of the 500 by way of the overhead passage which commands a superb bird's eye view of the huge hall. The suite was designed for Eleonora, Cosimo I's wife, by Vasari who, in 1562, renovated the apartments which originally served as the priors' residence. The small vestibule decorated with a *Virgin* attributed to Rossello di Iacopo Franchi leads to the **Sala Verde** (Green Room) which gets its name from the painted ceiling with the so-called grotesque style decoration by Ridolfo del Ghirlandaio. To the left is the **Studiolo di Eleonora** (Eleonora's Study) with a ceiling fresco by Salviati. To the right is the **Chapel** frescoed by Bronzino in the 1560s and one of the Mannerist artist's most ambitious undertakings. On the altar is a *Pietà* and an *Annunciation*. Along the walls are three stories from the life of Moses: the *Crossing of the Red Sea*, the *Bronze Serpent,* and *Moses making water flow from a rock*. From the Sala Verde we enter the apartments that Vasari rearranged for Eleonora. The ceilings were decorated by Bernardo del Tasso. The frescoes of episodes from the lives of famous women (after whom each room is named) were painted by Stradano after cartoons created by Vasari himself. The first room we see, the **Camera delle Sabine** (the Sabine Women Room), was assigned to Eleonora's ladies-in-waiting. The ceiling fresco shows the *Sabine women between the Roman and Sabine soldiers*. There are two paintings depicting the *Virgin and Child* on the wall, one by Lorenzo di Credi, the other by Andrea del Sarto. The portraits of young Medici are in the style of Sustermans, the Flemish master who took up residence in Florence. Next we come to the **Stanza di Ester** (Esther Room), or the Dining Room. The ceiling fresco of *Ahasuerus crowning Esther* is by Stradano. In addition there is a splendid carved marble basin. The **Stanza di Penelope** (Penelope's Room) has a panel of *Penelope at her loom* on the ceiling with other episodes from the Odyssey around the frieze. The view of Piazza della Signoria

Palazzo della Signoria — Hall of the Lilies.

from the windows is superb. Lastly, we come to the **Stanza della Bella Gualdrada** (the Room of the Fair Gualdrada) which was Eleonora's private chamber. On the ceiling is a fresco depicting *Gualdrada refusing to kiss Emperor Otto* while along the frieze are scenes of festivals held in Florence's main squares and streets. From here we enter a narrow passageway — in which Dante's death mask is displayed — leading to the **Cappella della Signoria** (Chapel of the Priors). This section of the building and the Hall of the 200 are all that remains of the Priors' Apartments dating from Florence's Republican period. The monk Girolamo Savonarola and his two followers spent the night before they were burned at the stake praying here. The frescoes are by Ridolfo del Ghirlandaio (1514), whereas the Holy Family on the altar is by Mariotto da Pescia. The **Audience Hall** with fine frescoes by Francesco Salviati (1550-1560) portraying scenes from the life of Camillus was designed by Benedetto da Maiano in the late 1400s. Particularly noteworthy is the carved marble and porphyry doorway surmounted by a statue of Justice also by a Maiano (1476-1478). The *wooden inlaid doors* with Dante and Petrarch effigied on them are by Giuliano da Maiano and Francione (1481). On the **Sala dei Gigli** (Lily Room) side of the doorway are statues of *St. John the Baptist* and little cupids, again by Maiano (1476-1478). The magnificent carved wooden ceiling is by Giuliano da Maiano. The walls are covered with a golden fleur-de-lis pattern on a blue ground (whence the name of the room) which stands for the alliance the Florentine Republic contracted with the Royal House of France. Facing the entrance is a huge fresco with illusionistic architecture by Domenico Ghirlandaio and his helpers (1481-1485). From left to right we see: *Brutus, Mutius Scaevola, Camillus, St. Zenobius between Sts. Laurence and Stephen, Decius, Scipio,* and *Cicero*. Donatello's bronze group of *Judith and Holophernes* (1460) has been placed in the Lily Room after being restored (1988). The door cut into the wall on the lefthand side leads to the **Chancellory**. The room has been dedicated to the most renowned of the Florentine chancellors, Machiavelli, of whom there are two portraits: a painted

Palazzo della Signoria — The Judith and Holophernes, by Donatello, after the 1988 restoration.

bust and a posthumous oil portrait painted in the late 16th century by Santi di Tito. The *Winged Cupid holding a dolphin* on a pedestal in the middle of the room is the original by Verrocchio (1476), once part of the main courtyard fountain, and moved here for preservation. Back in the *Sala dei Gigli*, the door beneath Ghirlandaio's frescoes, leads to the **Guardaroba Mediceo** or **Map Room** from the 33 maps painted on the cupboard doors by the famous mathematician, Fra Ignazio Danti (1563-1575) and Don Stefano Buonsignori (1575-1584). A door between the cupboards in the righthand corner of the room leads to a terrace from which you can view the oldest section of the building and reach the *"studiolo"* where Cellini used to repair the Medici jewelry. Leaving the *Sala dei Gigli* from the door on the right, we take the stairs to the passageway that skirts the outer part of the building. From here we get a magnificent panoramic view of the city. Climbing the tower, we reach the tiny cell dubbed *"L'alberghetto"* (the little hotel). From the top of the tower the view of Florence and the surrounding countryside is truly unforgettable. On the way down we can stop on the second floor, and, proceeding through the Hall of the Elements, we reach a series of 15 rooms containing an important collection of works of art recovered in Germany after World War II. See for instance: the *Crouching Aphrodite*, Roman sculpture, 2nd century A.D.; two fine coloured panels in *opus sectile*, 331 A.D.; Greek and Roman reliefs and sculptures of various epochs. Among the Medieval, Renaissan-

Palazzo della Signoria — The Medici Wardrobe or Map Room.

ce and later styles exemplified here, note: a beautiful little painting on wood of the *Madonna of Humility* attributed to Masolino and another very small *Madonna and Child* attributed to Masaccio; a large *Nativity* by Antoniazzo Romano; *Pygmalion and Galathea* by Bronzino; a fragment, barely rough hewn but very fine, of the *Rondanini Pietà* by Michelangelo; *Venus and Mercury present their son Anteros to Jove*, by Paolo Veronese; *Leda and the Swan*, by Tintoretto; *Portait of Elizabeth of Valois*, by Coelho; *Judith with the head of Holofernes* and a large *Equestrian portrait of Giovanni Carlo Doria* by Rubens; a beautiful *Portrait of an Unknown Man* by Hans Memling. On the mezzanine are the **Museum of Musical instruments**, containing rare and antique instruments of various periods, and the **Loeser Collection**, an important legacy of sculptures and paintings by Tuscan artists from the 14th to the 16th century. The most important works are: in sculpture, two terracotta groups representing soldiers and knights, by Giovanni Francesco Rustici (16th century); a splendid *Madonna and Child*, in painted wood, attributed to the school of Arnolfo di Cambio and a *marble Angel* by Tino da Camaino; in painting: the *Passion of Christ*, a curious work by Piero di Cosimo, end of 15th century: "an abstract and original spirit", Vasari called him in his *Lives*; a *Virgin and Child* by Pietro Lorenzetti (first half of 14th century) and the remarkable *Portrait of Laura Battiferri* by Agnolo Bronzino.

The Uffizi courtyard and porticos.

UFFIZI GALLERY

The Uffizi is not only the oldest art gallery in the world; it is the most important in Italy and also one of the greatest in Europe and in the whole world, visited by more than a million people every year. The gallery owns about 4800 works, of which about 2000 are on view (1000 paintings, 300 sculptures, 46 tapestries, 14 pieces of furniture and pottery, besides 700 more paintings kept in the Vasari corridor); the rest is in storage or on loan to other museums. This enormous quantity of works includes countless masterpieces, some being among the highest achievements of Western art. The building containing the Gallery was built for Cosimo I in

The Uffizi Gallery — Self-portrait, by Giorgio Vasari.

the mid 16th century in the area between Palazzo Vecchio and the Arno, to house the public offices (hence the name); the 11th century church of San Pietro Scheraggio, and the old Mint, where the Florentine currency (the florin) was coined, were partly incorporated. The planning was entrusted to Giorgio Vasari (the author of the *Lives of the artists* as well as court painter and architect), who built it between 1559 and the year of his death (and that of Cosimo), 1574; the building consists of two long porticoes joined by a third side that abuts on the Arno with a magnificent arch of great scenic effect. The outside of the Uffizi is reminiscent of Michelangelo's vestibule for the Laurentian Library: grey pietra serena architectural elements against gleaming white plaster. Together with the marvellous Corridor, it is Vasari's architectural masterpiece. Work on the

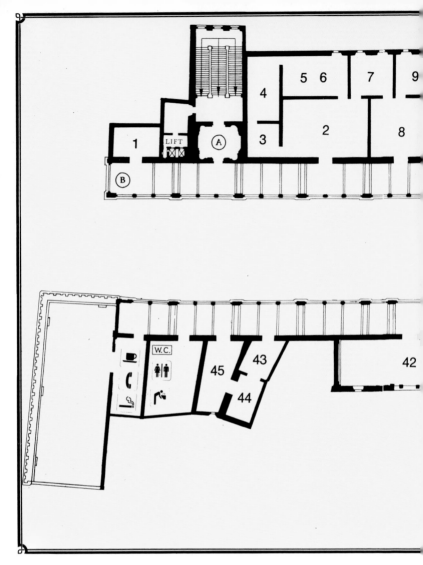

NOTE - The asterisks on the plan mark where the most important works in any particular room are hung and show the main stops along the itinerary of a visitor whose time is limited (1-2 hours).

1 — Classical Sculpture.
2 — Giotto and the 13th century.
3 — 14th century Sienese School.
4 — 14th century Florentine School.
5/6 — International Gothic Style.
7 — Early 15th century Florentine School.
8 — Filippo Lippi
9 — Pollaiolo.
10/14 — Botticelli.
15 — Leonardo da Vinci.

16 — Map Room.
17 — Room of the Hermaphrodite.
18 — The «Tribuna».
19 — Signorelli and Perugino.
20 — Dürer and the German School.
21 — Giovanni Bellini and Giorgione.
22 — Holbein and Altdorfer.
23 — Correggio and Mantegna.
24 — Miniature Collection.
25 — Michelangelo.
26 — Raphael and Andrea del Sarto.

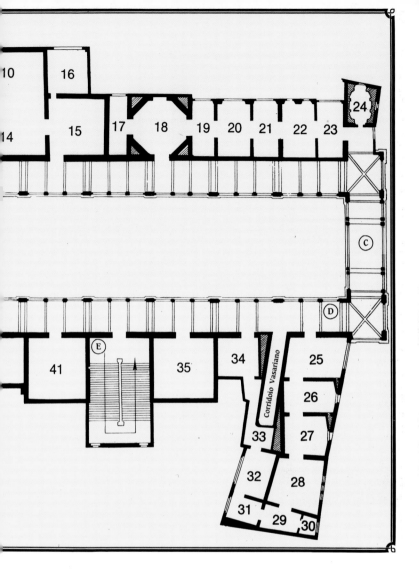

Apse of San Piero a Scheraggio, the church incorporated into the Uffizi
building.

Uffizi was resumed in 1580, by order of Francesco I, and directed by
Bernardo Buontalenti, who built the large Medici Theatre (dismantled in
1890) and the famous Tribuna; at the same time the top storey of the
loggia was restructured, the offices were transferred elsewhere and some
of the rooms were used for collections of works of art, arms, and scientific
curiosities; and so the Gallery was born. The first nucleus of works
already included paintings by Botticelli, Lippi, Paolo Uccello; about 1600
Ferdinando I had all the works at the Villa Medici in Rome transferred to
the Uffizi; in 1631 Ferdinando II contributed an important collection of
paintings (originally in Urbino: the inheritance of his wife Vittoria della
Rovere), including works by Piero della Francesca, Titian and Raphael; at
the end of the 17th century Cosimo II collected gems, medals and coins
and brought the *Venus*, later known as the "Medici" Venus, and other
important antique sculptures from Rome; Anna Maria Ludovica, Electress
Palatine, the last heir to the Medicis, enlarged the collection with Flemish
and German paintings and left it in its entirety to the state of Tuscany in
her will (1743). In the nineteenth century, after only part of the works of
art robbed during the Napoleonic wars had been restored and after the
creation of new specialised museums (Archaelogical Museum, Bargello,
Fra Angelico Museum, Silver Museum etc.) the Uffizi became what it is
today.

The Uffizi Gallery — Study of a man's head, by Michelangelo.

Past the ticket counters, we enter the recently restored church of **San Piero Scheraggio**, traversing the gangway, across the former crypt, on either side of which are Andrea del Castagno's renowned frescoed *Illustrious Men*. Originally painted for the Villa Pandolfini in nearby Legnaia (15th century), they are representations of well-known literary, mythological, and historical figures, from right to left: the Cuman Sibyl, Boccaccio, Petrarch, Dante, Farinata degli Uberti, Pippo Spano, Queen Esther, and Queen Tomiri. The second hall, on the site of the church's apse, contains traces of the original decoration as well as works by 14th century Tuscan painters. Sandro Botticelli's frescoed *Annunciation* graces the hall off to the right. The impressive staircase to the upper floors, designed by Vasari,

The Uffizi Gallery — First Corridor.

is decorated with sculptures of various periods, many of which are Roman copies of Greek originals. Off the second floor landing is the entrance to the **Gabinetto dei disegni e delle stampe** (Prints and Drawings Collection). This unique collection, started by Cardinal Leopoldo de' Medici, now comprises over 100,000 pieces by Italian and foreign artists.

The vestibule with antique statues on the third floor leads to the first wing of the picture gallery proper.

FIRST WING — The first gallery is the spacious loggia that Buontalenti restructured by order of Francesco I. On either side of the corridor are 4th-6th century A.D. Roman sarcophagi, as well as Roman busts and statues. The ceiling decoration, in the so-called grotesque style, is by Allori and other 16th century painters. The corridors are sometimes used to display some of the exquisite Flemish and Florentine tapestries in the Uffizi collection.

ROOM I — (At the beginning of the corridor) Roman and Greek sculpture.

78

The Uffizi Gallery — Enthroned Madonna and Child with Angels, by Giotto.

ROOM II — This is the hall of the 13th century Italian school. The works displayed here give the observant spectator a splendid chance to perceive how and when Italian painting started to break away from the stiffer, more schematic Byzantine tradition. The forerunners of what would be called the "Renaissance style" are Cimabue, here represented by a superb *Madonna and Child enthroned and Angels*, Duccio di Buoninsegna from Siena with his *Rucellai Madonna* (originally

79

The Uffizi Gallery — Annunciation, by Simone Martini and Lippo Memmi.

painted for the Rucellai Chapel in the Santa Maria Novella church), and perhaps the most revolutionary of all, Giotto, whose unique *Madonna and Child enthroned* is opposite the entrance. Generally dated 1303-1305, when Giotto was reputedly working on a fresco cycle in Assisi, this painting's naturalism and realistic approach to space and architecture is already a far cry from the schematic Byzantine figures flatly silhouetted against gold ground. In addition, there are works by 13th century artists from the school of Lucca: *St. Francis receiving the Stigmata*, a diptych with the *Virgin and Child surrounded by saints*, and a *Crucifixion* from the school of Bonaventura Berlinghieri. Also *St. Luke the Evangelist* by the Magdalen Master, the *Saviour amidst the Virgin and Saints* by Meliore di Jacopo, and a *Crucifix with scenes of the Passion*, Pisan school 12th century.

ROOM III — This room is filled with splendid examples of the especially refined style that typified 14th century Sienese art. They include major works by the Lorenzetti brothers, two of the foremost Sienese artists of the period: Ambrogio's *Circumcision*, the *Blessed Humility* and *Sts. John, Mark and Luke*. Perhaps the highlight amongst such treasures is Simone Martini's *Annunciation*, a veritable masterpiece of lyrical grace and refinement. In addition, there is a *Madonna and Child* by Niccolò di Sozzo Tegliacci, a *Nativity* by Simone de' Crocifissi, and a *Presentation at the Temple* by Niccolò Bonaccorsi.

ROOM IV — This room is dedicated to 14th century Florentine painters, especially followers of Giotto. These include Bernardo Daddi's *Madonna and Child* and

The Uffizi Gallery — The Battle of San Romano, by Paolo Uccello (detail).

Madonna and Child with Saints (two of the latter subject), Nardo di Cione's *Crucifixion*, Taddeo Gaddi's *Virgin in Glory*, and Giottino's *Deposition*.

ROOMS V-VI — The paintings here are typical examples of late 14th-early 15th century Italian painting. This particular blend of Giottoesque earthiness, Sienese refinement, plus a great profusion of elaborate ornamentations is known as the International Style, the so-called "flowery Gothic". The foremost International style painters are represented here: Gentile da Fabriano (*Adoration of the Magi* and *Four Saints*), Lorenzo Monaco (the huge *Coronation of the Virgin* and another *Adoration of the Magi*), Gherardo Starnina (the *Thebaid*), Agnolo Gaddi (*Crucifixion*), and Giovanni di Paolo (*Virgin and Child with Saints*). The three panels depicting *Scenes from the Life of St. Benedict* are by an unknown Northern Italian artist.

ROOM VII — Contains several famous masterpieces of 15th century painting: *Coronation of the Virgin* and *Virgin and Child* by Fra Angelico, *Virgin and Child surrounded by Saints* by Domenico Veneziano, and the *Virgin and St. Anne* by Masaccio and Masolino (Masaccio's teacher). Also Piero della Francesca's double portrait of *Federico da Montefeltro* and *Battista Sforza*. A whole wall is taken up by Paolo Uccello's *Battle of San Romano* which once hung in Lorenzo the Magnificent's bedroom in the Medici-Riccardi Palace.

ROOM VIII — 15th century paintings, mostly by Fra Filippo Lippi (a predella strip of *St. Fregidian deviating the Serchio River*; the *Annunciation of the death of the*

81

The Uffizi Gallery — Allegory of Spring, by Sandro Botticelli.

Virgin; *St. Augustine in his study*; the *Coronation of the Virgin*, which features fine portraits of several of Lippi's contemporaries; an altarpiece with the *Annunciation and saints*; the charming *Virgin and Child and two Angels*; an *Adoration of the Babe with St. Hilarion*; and another *Adoration with Sts. John and Romualdus*). Other painters represented are Alessio Baldovinetti (*Annunciation* and *Virgin and Child surrounded by Saints*), Lorenzo Vecchietta (*Virgin enthroned*), and Nicholas Froments (triptych depicting the *Resurrection of Lazarus*).

ROOM IX — The seated *Virtues* are by Antonio Pollaiolo, except for *Fortitude* by Botticelli. Antonio and Piero Pollaiolo, together, painted the fine portrait of *Galeazzo Sforza*. The *Portrait of a Youth with a red beret* is by Filippino Lippi, son of Filippo and pupil of Botticelli.

ROOMS X-XIV — This area is mostly devoted to works by the great master of line and colour, Sandro Botticelli, whose brillant grace typified 15th century Florentine painting; the most famous: the *Birth of Venus* and the *Allegory of Spring*, both impregnated with symbolic meanings; the *Madonna del Magnificat*; the *Calumny*; the *Annunciation*; the *Adoration of the Magi* and the *Portrait of a Young Man with a medallion*. The room also contains works by Rogier Van der Weyden, Ghirlandaio, Filippino Lippi, and Hugo Van der Goes' superb *Portinari Altarpiece*.

ROOM XV — Contains two famous works by Leonardo da Vinci: *The Annunciation* and the *Adoration of the Magi*, as well as a remarkable *Deposition* by Perugino and a recently restored *Crucifixion* by Signorelli.

ROOM XVI — Or the Map Room, frescoed with maps of Tuscany by Buonsignori.

ROOM XVII — This room is entered through the "Tribuna". Two important Hellenistic sculptures are here: *Amor and Psyche* and the famous *Sleeping Hermaphrodite* (2nd century B.C.).

82

The Uffizi Gallery — Allegory of Spring, by Sandro Botticelli (detail).

ROOM XVIII — The **"Tribuna"** was designed by Buontalenti c. 1589 as a showcase for the Medici's most treasured pieces. Standing in the middle is the renowned *Medici Venus*, a Greek masterpiece of the 3rd century B.C. The walls are hung with 16th century portraits by several of the best-known Mannerist painters (16th century). Two female portraits by Bronzino are especially handsome — *Eleonora di Toledo* and *Lucrezia Panciatichi*. There are also fine

The Uffizi Gallery — Birth of Venus, by Sandro Botticelli.

paintings by Rosso Fiorentino, Vasari, and Pontormo, not to mention the many pieces of Greek and Roman sculpture, inlaid furniture, and a mother-of-pearl dome.

ROOM XIX — The paintings in this room come from the Central Italian schools, including outstanding works by Perugino (portraits and a *Virgin between Sts. John the Baptist and Sebastian*) and by Luca Signorelli (the *Holy Family Tondo*, and a *Virgin and Child*, two of Signorelli's finest paintings). There is also a lovely *Annunciation* by Melozzo da Forlì and works by two painters greatly influenced by Perugino, Lorenzo Costa and Gerolamo Genga.

ROOM XX — Devoted to the German school, with several well-known paintings by one of the greatest German painters, Dürer: the *Calvary* (next to it is Brueghel's copy), portraits of *St. James the Greater* and *St. Philip the Apostle*, the *Adoration of the Magi*, *Portrait of the Artist's Father*, and a *Virgin and Child*. The *Portraits of Luther and His Wife*, *Luther and Melanchthon*, and *Adam and Eve* are by Lucas Cranach.

ROOM XXI — Dedicated to 15th century Venetian painting with an emphasis on Giorgione and Giovanni Bellini. The latter is represented by *Portrait of a gentleman*, *Sacred Allegory* (whose esoteric symbolism is made even more mysterious by the daylight setting), and the *Lamentation of Christ*. Giorgione's works are *Moses before Pharaoh* and the *Judgement of Solomon*. Also, paintings by other Northern Italian artists: the *Warriors and the Old Men*, by Carpaccio, *St. Louis of Toulouse* by Bartolomeo Vivarini, *Christ in the Temple* by Giovanni Mansueti, the delicate *Virgin and Child* by Cima da Conegliano, and *St. Dominic* by Cosmè Tura.

ROOM XXII — Paintings by Northern European Renaissance painters, such as Hans Holbein, the portrait painter (*Self-portrait and Portrait of Sir Richard*

The Uffizi Gallery — Overall view of the Tribuna; *below*: Wrestlers, 2nd century B.C. Greek.

The Uffizi Gallery — Second Corridor.

Southwell), Gerard David (the dramatic *Adoration of the Magi*). Lukas van Leyden (*Christ crowned with thorns*) and Albert Altdorfer (*Life of St. Florian*).

ROOM XXIII — Contains paintings by Antonio Allegri, better known as Correggio (1489-1534), who was greatly influenced by Leonardo. Correggio's hallmark, soft color and no contours, is evident in the works displayed here (the *Virgin in Glory*, the *Rest on the Flight to Egypt*, and the *Adoration*). The *Adoration of the Shepherds and the Madonna of the Quarries*, by Andrea Mantegna, are also here.

ROOM XXIV — Generally closed to the public, this room contains Italian and foreign miniatures from the 15th to 18th centuries.

SECOND WING — This section connects the two main corridors of the Uffizi. The works displayed are Roman sculptures. See: the *Boy removing a thorn from his foot*, *Venus*, two *Roman matrons*, and the *Girl preparing for the dance*. From the great western window in the second (shorter) gallery, one enjoys a splendid view of the Ponte Vecchio with the **Vasari corridor** running over it. Conceived as an aerial passage linking Palazzo Vecchio by means of a short bridge to the Uffizi, which are linked to the Grandducal residence of Palazzo Pitti by means of the Corridor proper. This singular feat of architecture and town planning was executed in the short space of five months, in 1565, by Giorgio Vasari,

The Vasari Corridor above the Old Bridge (Ponte Vecchio).

commissioned by Cosimo I. The Vasari Corridor starts from the Uffizi on the third floor between Room XXV and Room XXXIV, runs along the Arno over an arcade, Cross the river over Ponte Vecchio, passes between houses and palaces on the other side of the river, traverses the façade of the church of Santa Felicita, continues along the side of the Boboli Gardens and, after a distance of nearly a kilometre, enters the Pitti Palace. It was damaged in World War II and only reopened in 1973; one has to book visits in groups. About seven hundred paintings are on view, including 17th and 18th century Italian works, portraits of the Medici and the Hapsburgh grand dukes, and above all the famous **collection of self-portraits**, the most complete in the world, extending from the 14th

The Uffizi Gallery — The Doni Tondo or Holy Family, by Michelangelo.

century to the present time, including nearly all the greater Italian artists and numerous foreign ones.

THIRD WING — This corridor too is decorated with some fine Roman sculptures, mainly dating from the 2nd through the 4th century A.D. At the beginning are two statues of *Marsyas before his Flaying* (the one on the right was restored by Donatello). Further on are a *Discus-thrower*, *Leda and the Swan*, and other Greek mythological figures.

ROOM XXV — Displayed here among other masterpieces of 16th century paintings is one of Michelangelo's rare panel paintings, the so-called *Doni Tondo*, commissioned by Agnolo Doni. The subject is the Holy Family. See also a *Portrait of Perugino*, attributed to Raphael, as well as works by Rosso Fiorentino and Mariotto Albertinelli, two well-known Tuscan Mannerists.

ROOM XXVI — The Raphael room: the famous *Madonna del Cardellino*, *Leo X with Cardinals Giulio de' Medici and Luigi de' Rossi*, *Self-portrait*, and *Portrait of Francesco Maria della Rovere* are all here. In addition, Andrea del Sarto's *Madonna delle Arpie* (Virgin of the Harpies), not to mention fine works by

The Uffizi Gallery – The Venus of Urbino, by Titian.

Mannerists such as Pontormo (the *Martyrdom of St. Maurice*) and several portraits.

ROOM XXVII – This room is devoted to two of the foremost 16th century Mannerist painters, Bronzino and Pontormo. The *Holy Family*, *Lamentation of Christ*, and the refined *Portrait of a lady* are by Bronzino, whereas the *Supper at Emmaus*, the *Birth of St. John the Baptist*, *Portrait of a musician*, *Portrait of Maria Salviati*, and the *Virgin and Saints* were painted by Pontormo. There are also works by Franciabigio and Rosso Fiorentino.

ROOM XXVIII – This room is devoted to Titian (1477-1576) whose rich palette and emphatic use of light and shade became the hallmark of the Venetian school. Perhaps the best-known are the *Venus of Urbino*, the *Flora*, the *Portraits of Eleonora Gonzaga*, and *Francesca Maria della Rovere*, duke and duchess of Urbino, and *Venus and Cupid*. A follower of Titian's, Palma il Vecchio, painted the *Resurrection of Lazarus*, the *Holy Conversation*, and *Judith*.

ROOM XXIX – Several of Parmigianino's (1505-1540) finest works are hanging here: the *Virgin and Child with Saints*, a *Portrait of an Unknown Gentleman*, and the magnificent *Madonna dal Collo Lungo* (the Virgin with the long neck). Other artists represented are Ludovico Mazzolino, Luca Cambiaso, Scarsellino, and Girolamo da Carpi.

ROOM XXX – The painters represented here belong to the Central Italian Emilia-Romagna school. Mazzolino is represented by the *Circumcision of Christ* and the *Virgin and St. Anne*.

ROOM XXXI – Several works by Dosso Dossi, a Ferrarese artist greatly influenced by the Venetian school: *Portrait of a soldier*, the *Virgin in Glory*, and *Witchcraft*. Paintings by 16th century Venetian such as Lorenzo Lotto and Sebastiano del Piombo are also displayed.

The Uffizi Gallery — Still-life, by Rachel Ruysch.

ROOM XXXII — This room contains works by a prominent Venetian artist, Sebastiano del Piombo (1485-1547), known for his skillful fashion of modelling luminous colour into forms. A fine example is the *Death of Adonis* hanging here, by many considered his masterpiece. In addition, works by Lorenzo Lotto (*Sacra Conversazione*, *Susanna and the Elders*) and Paris Bordone (two portraits) are exhibited.

ROOM XXXIII — Also known as the "16th Century Hall" this passageway is hung with late 16th century Italian and foreign works including François Clouet's *Portrait of Francis I*, Alessandro Allori's *Portrait of Torquato Tasso*, Bronzino's *Allegory of Happiness*, and Jacopo Ligozzi's *Three Ages of Man*.

ROOM XXXIV — This room is devoted to Paolo Caliari better known as Veronese (1528-1588), one of the foremost 16th century Venetian school painters. Displayed are his *St. Agatha crowned by Angels*, the *Martyrdom of St. Justine*, the *Annunciation*, and the *Holy Family*. Other artists whose works hang here include Giulio Campi and Giovanni Battista Moroni, two prominent 16th century portrait painters.

ROOM XXXV — Here one can admire important works by Tintoretto (1518-1595) whose style is a combination of startling light and shade contrasts emphasizing intensely animated composition. The result is a uniquely dramatic effect that is typified in the *Good Samaritan*, the *Apparition of St. Augustine*, *Leda*, *Portrait of Jacopo Sansovino*, and *Portrait of a red-haired man*. The *Story of Joseph*, *Annunciation to the Shepherds*, and *Portrait of the Artist* are by another renowned 16th century Venetian artist, Jacopo Bassani. In addition, there are works by Federico Barocci and El Greco.

From Room XXXV you go directly to Room XLI as Rooms XXXVI to XL were eliminated when the *Buontalenti Staircase* was reopened.

ROOM XLI — Works by the Flemish masters Rubens and Van Dyck are here. Rubens' (1577-1640) impressive canvases of *Henry IV's triumphal entrance into Paris* and *Henry IV at the Battle of Ivry*, as well as two of his portraits, one of his wife *Isabel* and one of *Emperor Charles V* offer splendid insight into the Flemish painter's exuberant style. Anthony Van Dyck's portraits are incomparably skillful, as is Susterman's *Portrait of Galileo*.

ROOM XLII — The room, designed by Zanobi del Rosso, contains the group of *Niobe and her children*, a Roman copy of a Hellenistic IIIrd/IIrd century group, a neo-Attic *marble vase* (IIIrd/IIrd century A.D.) and a Roman *Rearing Horse*.

ROOM XLIII — The Caravaggio room, with the *Medusa*, *Bacchus* and the *Sacrifice of Isaac* by this great master of light and shade contrasts (1573-1610).

ROOM XLIV — Contains three magnificent works by Rembrandt van Rijn (1606-1669): two *Self-portraits* and a *Portrait of an old man*.

ROOM XLV — Among the paintings here are two charming *Views of Venice*, by Canaletto (1698-1768), a pair of *Capriccios* by Francesco Guardi (1712-1793) and two superb Goya *Portraits* (1746-1828).

The Uffizi Gallery — The mother of the Countess of Chinchon on horseback, by Francisco Goya.

THIRD ITINERAY

*Piazza della Repubblica — Loggia del Mercato Nuovo —
Via Por Santa Maria — Ponte Vecchio — Palazzo Pitti
(Palatine Gallery; Royal Apartments; Gallery of Modern
Art; Silver Museum; Coach Museum; Costume Museum;
Boboli Gardens) — Via Romana — Via Maggio — Church
of Santo Spirito — Church of Santa Maria del Carmine
(Brancacci Chapel).*

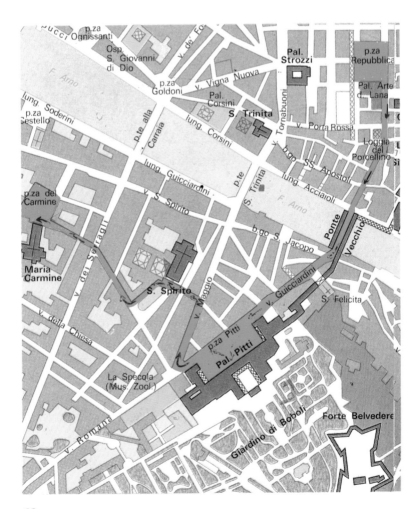

Piazza della Repubblica.

PIAZZA DELLA REPUBBLICA

In Roman times the city Forum stood where this piazza is today; there was a Temple of Jove and a column at the crossing of the two principal streets, *cardo* and *decumanus*, (respectively, the axis, Via degli Speziali - Via Strozzi, and Via Calimala - Via Roma). The Old Market, with its hovels, towers, loggias, stores and shops, all clustering round a column − known as the Column in the Market − on which was a statue of Plenty, replaced several times, superseded the Forum in medieval times. In the 19th century, after an epidemic of cholera, the Commune decided to "wipe out centuries of squalor", as the plaque over the archway reads, and pulled down the whole complex, replacing it with the pompous architecture of today's square.

From Piazza della Repubblica, along Via Pellicceria (the road with the porticos) one reaches the **Palagio dei Capitani di parte Guelfa** (the Palace of the Guelph Captains). The building stands in the small piazza of the same name, one of the

Palagio dei Capitani di Parte Guelfa (The Palace of the Guelph Captains) —
Exterior.

most picturesque places in medieval Florence. Built in the 14th century, it has a small, elegant façade with an outside staircase; it was enlarged in the 15th century (by Brunelleschi) and again by Vasari at the end of the 16th century. The powerful magistrature that it housed was established in 1267, when the Guelphs defeated the Ghibellines.

The Straw Market (Loggia del Mercato Nuovo) — Via Calimala just off Piazza Repubblica leads to the Straw Market, a Renaissance loggia with graceful arches on a raised platform designed by Giovanni del Tasso (1547-1551). Once, long ago the loggia served as Florence's bustling silk and gold trade center but nowadays people come here to buy straw, embroidery, lace, and other typical wares created by Florentine craftsmen. On the south side is a *fountain* with a statue of a wild boar on it known as *"il porcellino"* (piglet). The boar is a 17th century copy (by Pietro Tacca, 1612) of the Greek original in the Uffizi.

To the left of Via Por Santa Maria, the road connecting the Straw Market to the Ponte Vecchio, is the ancient church of **Santo Stefano al Ponte** in the little square named after the church, which has a simple Romanesque façade and a doorway decorated with marble in two colours (end of 13th century). The interior, with a single nave, was restored by Tacca in the 16th century; the structure of the unusual, highly elegant presbytery, preceded by a flight of steps by Buontalenti (1574) is flanked by a large altar on either side; there is a 16th century choir with a coffered ceiling: third altar on the left, bronze frontal with the *Martyrdom of St. Stephen*, by Tacca.

The Straw Market (Loggia del Mercato Nuovo); *below*: the fountain of the so-called piglet or «Porcellino», a bronze copy by Pietro Tacca from the Hellenistic original Boar in the Uffizi.

PONTE VECCHIO

As the name implies (Old Bridge), it is the oldest bridge in Florence: it has, in fact, existed since the time of the Roman colony, when the piers were of stone and the roadway of wood; destroyed by flooding in 1117 it was completely rebuilt in stone but collapsed again in the terrible flood of November 4th 1333; it was rebuilt for the last time in 1345 with three very wide spans, planned with room for shops on either side. First of all the butchers settled there (but later also grocers, smiths, shoemakers etc.); they built the picturesque shops projecting over the river, supported by struts and brackets. In 1591 Ferdinando I evicted them all only allowing the shops to the goldsmiths; and since then the bridge has been like two long jewellery-shop windows, only interrupted by the two clearings in the middle; the one looking downstream has a *bust of Benvenuto Cellini*, "master of the goldsmiths" by Raffaello Romanelli (1900).

Above and left, below: **the Old Bridge** (Ponte Vecchio); *top left:* **Bust of Benvenuto Cellini on the Ponte Vecchio.**

Leaving Ponte Vecchio and going along Via Guicciardini towards Piazza Pitti, we encounter the Church of **Santa Felicita** on our left, in its little square, built on the site of an early Christian basilica of the 4th century; several times rebuilt, the last time by Ruggieri in the 17th century. The Vasari Corridor runs across the façade of the church. The Medici family could attend services in the church from behind the gilded grate, having walked along the corridor from Palazzo Pitti without setting a foot out of doors. Inside, above the altar of the Capponi Chapel (first on the right) is a magnificent *Descent from the Cross* by Pontormo (c. 1528); on the right wall of the chapel a frescoed *Annunciation*, by Pontormo. In the elegant square sacristy (1470) designed by a follower of Brunelleschi's there are several noteworthy paintings such as a *Virgin and Child with Saints*, by Taddeo Gaddi, and *Santa Felicita and her seven children*, by Neri di Bicci.

At the end of Via Guicciardini, on the left-hand side, is an impressive mansion, **Palazzo Guicciardini**, for over five hundred years home of the famous Guicciardini family. It was built in the 15th century and restructured in the 1600s. The street terminates at Piazza Pitti, the huge square which serves as an appropriate setting for the magnificent Pitti Palace.

97

Pitti Palace — The façade.

PITTI PALACE

By the middle of the 15th century, the political control of the city was in the hands of the Medici family; Cosimo the Elder governed Florence from his new palace in Via Larga; Luca Pitti, at one time his friend, now led the faction that was most hostile to him and to his son Piero. Luca wanted a palace finer than the one that Michelozzo was building for the Medici. He chose the site, on the hill of Boboli, and commissioned Brunelleschi to design a building with windows as large as the doorways of the Medici palace and so large, that the Medici palace would fit into his courtyard. Brunelleschi accepted with alacrity (his own plan for Via Larga had been rejected at the time) and produced the plans about 1455. Work began in 1457 (after the master's death) under the direction of Luca Fancelli, Brunelleschi's pupil. The façade overlooking the piazza consisted only of the seven central windows; it was on three storeys separated by slender balconies and covered with rusticated stone. At the death of Luca Pitti in 1473 the palace was still incomplete; then the Pitti family fell into disfavour, and Eleonora of Toledo, the wife of Cosimo I, bought the building and the land behind it in 1549. In the 16th and 17th century this became the palace of the Medici, who enlarged it, created a garden on the Boboli hill, lengthened the building to nine windows each side, employing Giulio and Alfonso Parigi, and decorated the interior sumptuously. In the 18th century Ruggieri and Poccianti built the two porticoed side wings that enclose the piazza. The remarkable fact is that each successive

Pitti Palace seen from the Boboli Gardens.

enlargement substantially respected the original design by Brunelleschi, both in form and material. During the period in which Florence was the capital of Italy (1865-71) the palace was the residence of King Vittorio Emanuele II of Savoy. Since 1919it has been the property of the Italian State, together with its magnificent collections put together by generations of art-lovers. There are seven museums here: the **Palatine Gallery**, the **Monumental Apartments**, the **Silver Museum**, the **Gallery of Modern Art**, the **Gallery of Costumes**, the **Coach Museum** and the **Porcelain Museum**.

The main doorway leads into the majestic Ammannati courtyard (1558-1570), which is dominated by the *Artichoke Fountain* on the terrace above, on the garden side. There are two smaller fountains dedicated to Hercules, beneath the terrace, flanking the Moses Grotto, decorated with allegorical marble and porphyry statues. The staircase on the right leads up to the first floor where one enters the Palatine Gallery.

PALATINE GALLERY

SALA DI VENERE (Venus Room) — The ceiling was frescoed by Pietro da Cortona and Ciro Ferri and adorned with exquisite stuccowork by Roman artists (1641-1642). Several extraordinary paintings are hanging here, including Titian's renowned "*La Bella*", probably a portrait of Duchess Eleonora Gonzaga from Urbino, a *Sacra Conversazione* by Bonifacio de' Pitati, two *Seascapes* by Salvator Rosa, and *Portrait of Pietro Aretino*, one of Titian's late works. In addition, there is another Titian, a *Portrait of Julius II* which is a copy of a Raphael, to whom the

Palatine Gallery — The Venus Room.

painting was once attributed as a youthful work. The other Titian, the *Concert*, once attributed to his master, Giorgione, is now thought to be an early work, painted by Titian, while still in Giorgione's workshop. There are two Rubens: the *Peasants' return from the fields* and *Ulysses on the Isle of the Phaeacians*. Francesco Bassano painted the *Martyrdom of St. Catherine* and *Apollo and Marsyas* is by Guercino.

SALA DI APOLLO (Apollo Room) — The ceiling fresco is by Pietro da Cortona and Ciro Ferri (1647-1660). The series of great Titians continues here with the *Magdalen* and the *Portrait of the grey-eyed youth*. In addition, there is a superb Tintoretto: *Portrait of Vincenzo Zeno*, as well as a *Nymph chased by a satyr* and *St. John the Baptist* by Dosso Dossi, the *Holy Family* and a magnificent *Deposition*, by Andrea del Sarto, a splendid altarpiece by the Mannerist painter Rosso Fiorentino of the *Virgin and Saints*, a fine self-portrait by Andrea del Sarto, and lastly a double portrait by Anthony Van Dyck: *Charles I of England and Henrietta Maria* (his French Bourbon queen).

SALA DI MARTE (Mars Room) — The ceiling fresco was again painted by Pietro da Cortona and Ciro Ferri (1646). In addition to two charming versions of the *Virgin and Child* by the Spanish artist, Murillo, there are two major Rubens: a portrait group entitled the *Four Philosophers* (the first standing figure on the left is a self-portrait) and the renowned *Consequences of War*, a huge canvas painted by Rubens in Antwerp in 1638. Commissioned by Ferdinando II, the subject was inspired by the bloody Thirty Years' War. Two fine Titian portraits: *Ippolito de' Medici* and *Andrea Vesalio*, Van Dyck's *Portrait of Cardinal Bentivoglio* considered one of his finest, Tintoretto's *Portrait of Luigi Cornaro*, and Veronese's *Portrait of Daniele Barbaro*. Also works by Guido Reni and Guercino.

Palatine Gallery — Portrait of a lady (Venus Room) and Portrait of a gentleman
with grey eyes, both by Titian (Apollo Room); *below*: the Jupiter Room with the
statue of Victory, by Vincenzo Consani.

SALA DI GIOVE (Jupiter Room) — The mythological scenes on the ceiling are by Pietro da Cortona and Ciro Ferri (1643-1645). In the middle of the room is a marble statue of *Victory* by Vincenzo Consani (1867). One of Raphael's best-known paintings, *La Velata* (Lady with a veil) is here. The model who sat for the portrait was probably Raphael's mistress, *la Fornarina* (the baker girl), who often served as his model. Other fine paintings in the room: Borgognone's *Battle scene*, Andrea del Sarto's *Portraits of the artist and his wife* and his charming *Annunciation*, Bronzino's *Portrait of Guidobaldo della Rovere*, Fra Bartolomeo's striking *Deposition* and Perugino's *Madonna of the Sack*

SALA DI SATURNO (Saturn Room) — The ceiling fresco by Ciro Ferri (1663-1665) is based upon a design by Pietro da Cortona. This room contains a number of Raphael's major works, including the much loved *Madonna of the Chair*, where the figures' full, rounded forms belong to the artist's Roman period; the Portrait of *Cardinal Dovizi da Bibbiena*; the unfinished *Madonna del Baldacchino* (Virgin of the *Canopy*); and the Wedding portraits of *Agnolo and Maddalena Doni*. Also the famous *Madonna del Granduca* of 1505. A subtle blend of Leonardesque and Umbrian influences (Raphael's early style developed in Umbria where he studied under Perugino). Also here: Perugino's *Deposition* painted in Florence in 1495 and the *Magdalen*, with its intense light and shade contrasts. Also: Ridolfo del Ghirlandaio's portrait of a *Goldsmith* and Guercino's *St. Sebastian*.

SALA DELL'ILIADE (Iliad Room) — The ceiling decoration by Luigi Sabatelli portrays episodes from Homer's Iliad. The statue in the middle by Lorenzo Bartolini (1824) represents *Charity*. The highlights of the room are Velasquez's Portrait of *Philip IV of Spain*, a series of end of the 16th — beginning of the 17th

Palatine Gallery — The Veiled Lady, by Raphael (Jupiter Room) and the Madonna of the Grand Duke, by Raphael (Saturn Room).

Palatine Gallery — **The expectant mother, by Raphael** (Iliad Room) **and the Lost Drachma, by Domenico Feti** (Poccetti Gallery).

century portraits, by Justus Sustermans, the official portrait painter to the Medici court at the time, and a Portrait of *King Philip II of Spain* by Titian, also two *Assumptions* by Andrea del Sarto and Raphael's portrait of a Lady known as *La Gravida* (the pregnant woman) painted in Florence when Raphael was still influenced by Leonardo.

SALA DELL'EDUCAZIONE DI GIOVE (Room of the Education of Jupiter) — (To the right of the Sala dell'Iliade). The room was named after the mythological of the ceiling fresco by Luigi Catani (1819). The paintings displayed are a striking *Portrait of a man* by Van Dyck, Caravaggio's famous *Sleeping Cupid*, a *Pietà* by Francesco Salviati, and the *Chaste Susanna* by Guercino. The head of Holofernes in Cristoforo Allori's *Judith* is supposedly a self-portrait of the artist.

SALA DELLA STUFA (Room of the Stove) — The walls and ceiling of this room are entirely frescoed by Matteo Rosselli and Pietro da Cortona with the allegorical scenes of the Golden, Silver, Bronze and Iron Ages.

SALETTA DA BAGNO (Bathroom) — The neo-Classical decorative scheme of stuccowork and bas-reliefs is by Giuseppe Cacialli.

SALA DI ULISSE (Ulysses Room) — The ceiling fresco by Gaspare Martellini depicting *Ulysses' return to Ithaca* was meant to symbolize Ferdinando III's return to Florence after Napoleon's defeat. There are several paintings by the 17th century painter Carlo Dolci (the *Virgin and Child* is especially charming). Cigoli's *Ecce Homo*, Tintoretto's *Portrait of Andrea Frazier*, Filippino Lippi's *Death of Lucretia*, Raphael's *Madonna dell'Impannata* (*impannata* indicates the oiled cloth on the window) and a *Portrait of Alfonso di Ferrara* attributed to Titian.

SALA DI PROMETEO (Prometheus Room) — The frescoed ceiling and frieze, by Giuseppe Collignon (1842), depict scenes from the myth of Prometheus. The

Palatine Gallery — The Madonna of the Chair, by Raphael (Saturn Room).

paintings in the room include Pontormo's *11,000 martyrs*, Albertinelli's *Holy Family* and Luca Signorelli's treatment of the same subject, Filippo Lippi's charming tondo of the *Virgin and Child* and Francesco Botticini's *Virgin and Child with Angels*.

POCCETTI GALLERY — The ceiling was frescoed by Bernardo Poccetti (16th cent.). There two portraits by Rubens, *Ila and the nymphs* by Francesco Furini, the *Martyrdom of St. Bartholomew* by Ribera, four *landscapes* by Poussin, and the *Missing drachma* by Domenico Feti.

SALA DELLA MUSICA (Music Room) — It is also known as the Drum Room from

Palatine Gallery — The Iliad Room.

the drum-shaped furniture. The table in the middle is made of Russian malachite and has gilded bronze supports by Thomire.

SALA CASTAGNOLI — The room was named after the painter who decorated it in the 19th century. The round *table* in the middle is inlaid with precious stones. Made in Florence in 1851, and known as the "Table of the Muses" it shows Apollo in his chariot surrounded by symbols of Muses. The bronze support with *Seasons and cupids* is by Giovanni Duprè.

SALA DELLE ALLEGORIE (Allegory Room) — The room is also known as "Sala del Volterrano" (Volterrano is the name of the painter who frescoed the allegorical scenes). The paintings include the *Pranks of Pievano Arlotto*, *Profane Venus*, and *Sleeping Cupid* also by Volterrano, the *Virgin and Child* by Artemisia Gentileschi, as well as *Venus and Amor* and the *Wedding Night* by Giovanni da San Giovanni.

SALA DELLE ARTI (Art Room) — Frescoed by Podestà (19th century). Paintings by Doldi, Ligozzi, and Rustici, and an *Adoration of the Magi* by Cristoforo Allori.

SALA DI ERCOLE (Hercules Room) — Pietro Benvenuti frescoed the *Stories of Hercules* in the neo-Classical style. Also a splendid *Sèvres vase*, a present from Napoleon to Ferdinand III.

SALA DELL'ARCA (Ark Room) — Frescoed in 1816 by Luigi Ademollo to represent the pavilion David built for the Ark.

CAPPELLA DELLE GRANDUCHESSE (the Chapel of the Grandduchesses, also known as the Reliquary Chapel) — Decorated with gilded stuccowork and frescoes, in the early 17th century for Maria Magdalen of Austria as a private chapel for the grandduchess.

Palatine Gallery — The Table of the Muses (Castagnoli Room).

THE ROYAL APARTMENTS

These magnificent apartments were the living quarters of the Medici, the Hapsburg granddukes, and in the 19th century, of the Savoy family, the Italian sovereigns.

The first room, or Dining Hall is also called the SALA DELLE NICCHIE (Niches Room).

SALA VERDE (Green room) is hung with Gobelins tapestries. The allegorical frescoes honouring the Medici are by Luca Giordano.

SALA DEL TRONO (Throne room) contains the throne on which the kings of Italy took oath. The room contains portraits by Sustermans and François Pourbus.

SALA CELESTE (Blue Room) is decorated with Gobelins tapestries, portraits by Sustermans, and rare Chinese vases.

The CHAPEL with portraits of Medici Cardinals by Sustermans.

The SALA DEI PAPPAGALLI (Parrot Room) was named for the parrot motifs in the tapestries. There are paintings by Titian (*Portrait of the Duchess of Urbino*) and Hans von Aachen (*Portrait of Francesco I*). This room and the following two were Queen Margherita of Italy's Suite. The SALA GIALLA (Yellow Room), is hung with Gobelins tapestries, as well as portraits, one, attributed to J.F. Douven depicting the *Electress Palatine*.

Back in the Sala dei Pappagalli, we enter King Umberto I's suite. The bedroom, study, and living room are decorated with tapestries and portraits. The SALA DI BONA was frescoed by Poccetti with scenes showing the *Conquest of the city of*

The Royal Apartments — Throne Room.

Bona in Africa, the *Conquest of Prevesa, a View of Leghorn harbor*, and an *Apotheosis of Cosimo I.*

SALA BIANCA (White Room), the ballroom's ceiling and walls are covered with Neo-classical stuccos. Beautiful chandeliers. Used by the Hapsburgs and the Savoy Sovereigns for official receptions.

THE GALLERY OF MODERN ART

Situated on the last floor of the palace, it is reached by the staircase right of the main entrance, which also leads up to the Palatine Gallery. Founded by the Tuscan provisional government in 1860, this museum contains a fascinating Italian 19th century collection. In addition to the neo-Classical and academic schools profusely represented, there are also numerous paintings belonging to a Tuscan movement called "I Macchiaioli" (from macchia = splash or mark) which was akin and contemporary but not influenced by the French Impressionist Movement. The "Macchiaioli" artists strove to free themselves from the restrictions and conventions of academic art, seeking for inspiration in nature and reality. Works by the head of the movement, Giovanni Fattori, and of all its major exponents: Silvestro Lega, Telemaco Signorini, Giuseppe Abbati, Raffaele Sernesi, may be viewed. There are also works by artists alive today. Of especial interest: *The solemn entry of Charles VIII into Florence*, by Giuseppe Bezzuoli; *Il convicts' penitentiary in Portoferraio*, by Telemaco Signorini; *The duke of Athens' expulsion*, by Stefano Ussi; *The Usurer*, by Domenico Induno; *The Palmieri Rotonda*, by Giovanni Fattori.

THE SILVER MUSEUM

Instituted in 1919 and arranged on the ground floor of Pitti Palace, in the rooms that were used as the summer apartments of the Grand Dukes. The core of this

Modern Art Gallery — The Usurer, by Domenico Induno and Jack La Bolina's daughter, by Vittorio Corcos.

priceless collection of silver, gemstones, jewels, ivories, china, glassware, and textiles was put together by the Medici family and then further increased by the addition of the Electress Palatine's treasury and bequests by the Savoys and private citizens. Space does not permit us to list each and every object on display; only the higlights will be described.

SALA DI GIOVANNI DA SAN GIOVANNI — Once the antechamber to the grandukes' summer suite, the room was frescoed between 1638 and 1642 by Giovanni di San Giovanni and his pupils. The subject of the frescoes is Lorenzo the Magnificent giving refuge to the Muses after they have been chased from Mt. Parnassus. The ceiling fresco is an allegorical representation of the marriage of Grandduke Ferdinand II to Vittoria della Rovere.

THE CHAPEL — The chapel was frescoed between 1623 and 1634.

SALA DELL'UDIENZA (Audience Hall) — The frescoes were painted between 1636 and 1641 by the Bolognese artists Colonna and Mitelli. The 17th century ebony *stipo* cabinet inlaid with precious stones was a gift from Archduke Leopold of Tyrol to Ferdinando II in 1628.

SALA DELL'UDIENZA PRIVATA (Private Audience Hall) — The frescoes are by Colonna and Mitelli.

THE THIRD SALA DI RAPPRESENTANZA (Third Audience Hall) — The frescoes are once again by Colonna and Mitelli. From this room we enter (on the right) a section comprising four rooms and, up a little staircase a further series of mezzanine rooms, called the *Treasury* (Tesoro). Here displayed in showcases are objects from various schools and periods which are tangible proof of the incredible level the so-called minor arts reached between the 16th and 18th centuries. The highlights include French, German, and Flemish 17th century ivories (especially the ivory *chalices* from Coburg crafted for the Duke of Saxony) several pieces by Balthazar Stockamer, and a 16th century Flemish carved *Crucifixion* once owned

109

by Pope Pius V. In addition, see also the *statuettes of the Apostles* by Orazio Mochi, the *lapis-lazuli vase* crafted for Francesco I de' Medici after a design by Buontalenti, an engraved crystal *goblet* with gold-plated lid engraved and enamelled with the emblems of Henry II of France and Diane of Poitiers, a painting showing *St. Anne teaching the Virgin to read* by Solimena (late 16th-early 17th century), with a fine silver frame, as well as a vast array of reliquaries, cameos, vases, statuettes, and gold table-ware.

THE COACH MUSEUM

(The entrance is beneath the arcade of the right wing of the palace). This fascinating little museum contains the carriages in use from the 16th to the 19th centuries, as well as fittings and costumes dating from various periods. In the entrance hall are precious fittings that once belonged to the Medici court in the 18th century. The second room contains the exhibition of coaches, among which is the sedan belonging to the Electress Palatine Maria Luisa (18th century), the coaches belonging to the Duke of Modena, Francesco II (17th century), the Grandduke of Tuscany, Leopoldo II (1815); the King of Naples, Ferdinando (1839); Caterina de' Medici (16th century), as well as the special chair Grandduke Cosimo II used for going up and down stairs, after his legs were paralyzed.

Back in the square, one goes throught the left wing gateway (the Arno river side), leading into the Boboli Gardens.

THE COSTUME MUSEUM

The museum consists of about 15 rooms in the Pavilion of the "Meridiana" (the long, low building to the left of Pitti Palace (looking from the gardens). It was

The Meridiana Pavilion (the Costume Museum).

Boboli Gardens — The Fountain of Oceanus, by Giambologna.

instituted in 1983 and is intended to illustrate the evolution of dress and costume in Italy from the 18th to the present century, with particular emphasis on the fashions of the 19th century. The collection is continually being added to, thanks to generous donations and every two years there is a special exhibition of the latest costumes that have joined the collection. The costumes, both male and female, beautifully preserved and restored, are exhibited in the fascinatingly furnished and decorated rooms of the Pavilion (most of the furnishings are 18th and 19th century). All the lovely, unique costumes are worn by specially structured dummies, made to fit them and protected by transparent cases, whilst the corresponding accessories (shoes, hand-bags, hats, gloves, umbrellas, etc.) are carefully displayed in show-cases. One of the rooms contains a delightful collection of fashion-prints, reviews and books on dress and costume.

BOBOLI GARDENS

The gardens were laid out on the Boboli hill shortly after Pitti Palace became the property of Cosimo I and Eleonora of Toledo, towards the second half of the 16th century. Michelangelo's pupil, the architect and sculptor Niccolò Pericoli, called "Tribolo", was given the task of designing a garden in accordance with the new Renaissance mode, which exacted more stately proportions than the Medieval private "viridarium" (or

The Boboli Gardens — The Bacchus Fountain, by Vittorio Cioli.

greenery) had accustomed people to. A Renaissance garden was the symbol of a prince's power, the scene of parties and plays, a place of relaxation for the court, where one could wander through groves populated by allegorical statues, grottoes, fountains. Boboli underwent many alterarions owing to variations in taste, but the design remained substantially the same.

Near the entrance to the left of the palace, on the Piazza Pitti side, is the curious *Bacchus Fountain* in which Valerio Cioli portrayed a dwarf of the court of Cosimo I

The Boboli Gardens — The Amphitheatre; *below*: two views of the gardens.

The Boboli Gardens — The gate leading into the Oceanus fountain enclosure.

astride a tortoise; further on is the *Grotto by Buontalenti*, built between 1583 and 1588 for the eccentric Francesco I; the first chamber is like a real cave and decorated with sculptured forms that, on closer examination, look like animals; in the corners are four copies of Michelangelo's *Prisoners* (Accademia Gallery) which used to be here; in the cave behind, the group of *Paris and Helen*, by Vincenzo de' Rossi; last comes a small grotto with a *Venus* by Giambologna. Returning towards the entrance, a gravel path leads up to the 17th century *Amphitheater* with a gigantic granite basin in the middle moved here from the Baths of Caracalla in Rome and flanked by an Egyptian obelisk. From the Amphitheater we climb the hill to the *Neptune Garden* named after the bronze statue of *Neptune* by Stoldi in the middle of the pool. Turning left here we reach the *Belvedere Fortress* which offers a delightful view of the city and the hills of Fiesole. Returning to the giant basin we climb up to the statue of *Abundance* by Giambologna and Tacca. Turning right we reach the *Giardino del Cavaliere* (The Garden on the saddle of the hill) where we encounter the **Porcelain Museum**. If we take the ramp on the left we come to a pleasant meadow surrounded by cypresses and holm-oaks called the *Prato dell'Uccellare*. This is the beginning of the broad path leading to the *Piazzale dell'Isolotto* with Giambologna's *Fountain of Oceanus* in the center. By way of the *Limonaia* (lemon shelter) we reach the exit on Via Romana.

114

The Boboli Gardens – The Porcelain Museum; *below*: the Lemon-tree Shelters (Limonaia).

Via Romana – The exit of the Boboli Gardens leads into Via Romana. Before continuing our intinerary (which from here should go right), we shall take a brief excursion to the left. Via Romana ends at Porta Romana, a massive cropped tower built in 1326. Inside the arch is a fresco by Franciabigio of a *Virgin and Child and four saints*. The road running left of the *piazzale* is the beginning of Viale dei Colli, divided into three sections named after Machiavelli, Galilei and Michelangelo, a splendid winding drive that skirts the city, passing the panoramic terrace known as Piazzale Michelangelo. The tree-lined road to the right of Viale Machiavelli leads, instead, to the *Villa di Poggio Imperiale*, a very old building which was enlarged by Giulio Parigi in 1620 and was later restructured several times. Today it is a private school for girls.

Going back to our itinerary, we pick up where we left off at the exit of the Boboli Gardens on Via Romana.

Number 17 Via Romana is the **Specola Natural History Museum**, founded by Peter Leopold, the Hapsburgh-Lorraine Grandduke. The museum's 36 rooms contain over 2,000,000 insects, 90,000 vertebrates, 15,000 reptiles, 20,000 birds, 37,000 fish, 11,000 mammals, and so on. In addition, there is a fascinating collection of remarkable anatomical models of coloured wax. The collection totals over 1400 of these rigorously accurate models produced in the 18th and 19th centuries by various authors. The interesting **Tribuna of Galileo** by Giuseppe Martelli on the second floor was built on occasion of the third symposium of scientists held in Florence, by Giuseppe Bezzuoli and Luigi Sabatelli with scenes from the life of the great scientist. For exaple, Galileo is shown as he observes the oscillations of the lamps in the Cathedral of Pisa which led him to formulate the law of the isochronism of the pendulum. Lower down, he is presenting a telescope to the Doge of Venice, and finally, old and blind, he is dictating the law of falling masses to his pupils Torricelli and Viviani. The tribuna is generally closed to the public but is visible upon request.

Some yards further on the street opens onto Piazza San Felice. On the left is the **church of San Felice**, with a façade by Michelozzo (1457) and a fine carved Renaissance portal. The aisleless interior is adorned with several remarkable paintings; a 14th century *Pietà* by Niccolò di Pietro Gerini (first righthand altar), *Virgin and Child with saints* by Rodolfo del Ghirlandaio (fifth altar), *St. Felix coming to the aid of St. Maximus* by Giovanni da San Giovanni (seventh left-hand altar) and a *Crucifixion* in the choir by a follower of Giotto.

Via Maggio – Via Maggio, the middle street branching out of Piazza San Felice, was actually once called Via Maggiore (Greatest Street) – indeed it was a very wide street for the times. It is lined with aristocratic mansions built between the 14th and 17th centuries. Number 8, *Casa Guidi*, is the house that Elizabeth Barrett Browning lived and died in (1861). Above the door is an inscription composed by the Italian writer Niccolò Tommaseo to commemorate her. Number 26, the 16th century *Palazzo Buontalenti*, was the home of Bianca Cappello, mistress and second wife of Francesco Ist de' Medici. There are several other interesting buildings along the way: Number 43, *Casa Ridolfi* (14th century); Number 50, *Casa Rosselli del Turco* (15th century); Number 42, *Palazzo Corsini* (15th century); and Number 30, *Palazzo Biliotti*.

Retracing our steps to Piazza San Felice we turn into the sidestreet, Via Mazzetta, leading to Piazza Santo Spirito, one of the most attractive squares in Florence; Number 10 is **Palazzo Guadagni**, an outstanding Florentine Renaissance palace, attributed to Cronaca (1503-1506). The building is surmounted by a graceful loggia and sports a lovely wrought-iron lantern on the corner.

The Church of Santo Spirito overlooking its shady square.

SANTO SPIRITO

Santo Spirito was built on the site of a 13th century church, part of an Augustinian monastery. One of the finest of the Early Renaissance buildings, it was begun by Brunelleschi in 1444 and continued by Antonio Manetti and Salvi d'Andrea until its completion in 1487. The graceful belltower on the north side was designed by Baccio d'Angelo. The dome, designed by Brunelleschi, was built by Salvi d'Andrea.

THE INTERIOR — The effect of the slender columns and graceful arches along both aisles and the transept is extremely elegant. The 38 semi-circular chapels used to contain a considerable number of paintings, but many have since been moved elsewhere. Following is a list of the church's major attractions. Right aisle: In the end chapel: a 16th century copy (by Baccio Bigio) of Michelangelo's *Pietà* in St. Peter's. In the 3rd chapel: a wooden statue of *St. Nicholas of Tolentino* attributed to Nanni Ungaro. In the 6th chapel: the *Martyrdom of St. Stephen* by Passignano. The Baroque main altar (1608) with an elaborate tabernacle is by Giovanni Caccini. Right transept: in the 4th chapel on the 15th century altar: a *Virgin and Child with St. John and other saints*, also known as the Tanai Altarpiece from the name of the family that commissioned it, by Filippo Lippi (c. 1490). The elaborate frame is contemporary to the painting. In the 7th chapel behind the bronze grating: the *tomb of Neri Capponi* by Bernardo Rossellino (1458). Apse: in the 1st chapel: a *Virgin with Saints* attributed to Raffaello de' Carli. In the 2nd chapel: a *Virgin and Child with saints* by a pupil of Bernardo Daddi. In the 4th chapel: a painting of *Martyrs* by Alessandro Allori. The predella panel below has a view of Palazzo Pitti before it was enlarged. In the 5th chapel: the *Woman taken in Adultery* also by Alessandro Allori. In the 7th chapel: a 15th

117

Santo Spirito — Interior.

century Florentine school *Annunciation*. In the 8th chapel: a *Nativity* by a pupil of Ghirlandaio. Left transept: its 15th century appearance is more or less intact. First chapel: *St. Monica founding the Augustinian Order*, painting by Botticini. 2nd chapel: *Virgin and Child with saints* by Cosimo Rosselli (1482). Fourth chapel: the entire marble ornamentation is an early work by Andrea Sansovino. The railing, dated 1642, is also worthy of note. 5th chapel: *Holy Trinity* by Francesco Granacci. 7th chapel: *Virgin and Child with saints* by Raffaellino del Garbo (1505). 8th chapel: *St. Thomas* by Michele del Ghirlandaio. Left aisle (starting from the left arm of the transept): 1st chapel: *Virgin enthroned with saints* by Fra Bartolomeo; 3rd chapel: *Virgin, St. Anne, and other saints* by Ridolfo and Michele del Ghirlandaio; 6th chapel: a copy of Michelangelo's *Christ carrying the Cross* by Taddeo Landini (the original is in Santa Maria sopra Minerva in Rome). At the third bay a door beneath the organ opens into the **vestibule** built by Cronaca in 1494 with barrel vaults resting upon twelve Corinthian columns. The vestibule leads into the lovely octagonal **sacristy** designed by Giuliano da Sangallo.

The Refectory – The entrance is to the left of the church façade. The collection includes medieval and Renaissance (11th-15th century) sculpture bequeathed to the city by a Florentine art collector, Salvatore Romano. On the wall of the great hall which once served as the refectory (cenacolo) of the Augustinian monks is a huge fresco of the *Last Supper* and the *Crucifixion* by Andrea Orcagna and his helpers (c. 1360). Several detached frescoes dating from the 14th century are also displayed in the hall.

Crossing the square, we turn right into Via Sant'Agostino, cross Via de' Serragli, and continue down Via Santa Monica until we come to Piazza del Carmine.

Santa Maria del Carmine — The Brancacci Chapel frescoed Tribute scene by Masaccio.

SANTA MARIA DEL CARMINE

First begun in 1268 when the Romanesque style was starting to be influenced by the new Gothic lines. The church was extensively restructured during the 16th and 17th centuries. In 1771 it was almost completely burnt down in a fire, but miraculously the famous Brancacci and Corsini chapels survived unscathed. Between 1771 and 1775 it was rebuilt by Giuseppe Ruggeri and Giulio Mannaioni in the Baroque style, although the façade was left unfinished.

INTERIOR — The ground plan is a Latin cross, opening onto numerous side-chapels. The 18th century frescoes decorating the vault above the nave and the transept are by Domenico Stagi and Giuseppe Romei. Above the third altar on the right: *Crucifixion*, by Giorgio Vasari. At the end of the right transept, is the **Brancacci Chapel**, the frescoes of which influenced the whole of Western painting in a most fundamental fashion. The chapel was built at the end of the 14th century and, starting in 1425 (commissioned by the rich Florentine merchant and envoy Felice Brancacci) was totally covered with frescoes. The artist first entrusted with the task was Masolino da Panicale, who was still influenced by the Gothic style, but was also aware of the new innovative trends that were already abroad in the Tuscan artistic scene of the time. The herald of this new line of thought was to be Tommaso di Ser Giovanni, called Masaccio, the young helper Masolino chose to assist him in the decoration of the Brancacci chapel. Masaccio was to take over from his old master, but for reasons as yet unknown never

119

Santa Maria del Carmine — Overall view of the Brancacci Chapel.

finished the task. The frescoes were in effect only finished between 1481 and 1485 by Filippino Lippi. It was however, in the Brancacci chapel that Masaccio was to paint his greatest masterpieces: the figures possess an overwhelming naturalistic and dramatic quality, all superfluous ornamentation is rigorously absent and one is irresistibly reminded of Giotto. These figures were to qualify Masaccio (who unfortunately died when he was barely twentyseven years old) as the first great painter of the Renaissance. The two cycles that decorate the chapel describe episodes from the Stories of the Original Sin and the Life of St. Peter the Apostle. Starting from the top of the left wall the scenes are: 1) *Adam and Eve expelled from the Garden of Eden*, by Masaccio; 2) *The payment of the tribute*, by Masaccio; 3) *The preaching of St. Peter*, by Masolino; to the right of the altar: 4)

The Church of San Frediano in Cestello.

St. Peter christens the neophytes, by Masaccio; 5) the left side of the fresco with *St. Peter healing the cripple* is by Masaccio, while the right side, with *St. Peter resuscitating Tabitha*, is by Masolino; 7) *Temptation of Adam*, by Masolino. On the lower level from the left: 8) *St. Paul visiting St. Peter in prison*, by Filippino Lippi; 9) the left side of the fresco with *St. Peter resuscitating the grandson of the Emperor*, was started by Masaccio and finished by Filippino Lippi; 10) the right side with *St. Peter preaching from a pulpit* is by Masaccio; 11) *St. Peter healing the sick with his shadow*, by Masaccio; 12) *St. Peter and St. John giving alms*, by Masaccio; 13) *St. Peter is condemned and crucified*, by Filippino Lippi; 14) *The angel delivers St. Peter from prison*, by Filippino Lippi. The vault of the chapel is frescoed by Vincenzo Meucci (1765) and shows the *Virgin giving a scapular to the Blessed Simon Stock*. – The **Sacristy** is also of great interest: entrance to the left of the Brancacci Chapel. It contains various 14th and 15th century works, including a polyptych by a follower of Andrea Bonaiuti (or da Firenze), depicting a *Madonna and Child with Saints*, as well as a *Crucifix* by a follower of Cimabue. At the end of the left arm of the transept, is the Baroque **Corsini Chapel**, by Francesco Silvani (1675-1685). The frescoes in the vault are by Luca Giordano.

Back in the square, one crosses it lengthwise and turns left into Borgo San Frediano, which leads on to the **Church of San Frediano in Cestello**, which was built in 1689 by Antonio Ferri, who was also responsible for the fine dome.

FOURTH ITINERARY

Piazza del Duomo – Via dei Cerretani – Via Tornabuoni – Palazzo Strozzi – Piazza Santa Trinita (Church of Santa Trinita) – Lungarno Corsini (Corsini Gallery) – Cascine Park – Ognissanti Square and Church – Piazza Santa Maria Novella (Church and Cloisters of Santa Maria Novella).

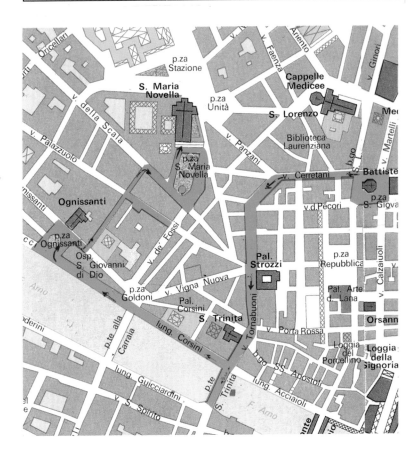

Via dei Cerretani — One of the busiest thoroughfares in the city, this street goes from Piazza del Duomo to the main railway station. A few yards from Piazza del Duomo it passes the **church of Santa Maria Maggiore** (entrance on the little square around the corner). First built in the 10th century, it was later rebuilt at the end of the 1200s. Above the main doorway is a statue of the *Virgin and Child* (14th century Pisan school). Inside, is the tomb of *Brunetto Latini*, Dante's master. In the chapel to the left of the choir is a 13th century painted relief of the

122

Looking down Via Tornabuoni.

Virgin enthroned attributed to Coppo di Marcovaldo. Continuing down Via dei Cerretani, we turn left into Rondinelli which in turn leads into **Piazza Antinori** The square takes its name from the elegant 15th century **Palazzo degli Antinori** on the right, attributed to Giuliano da Maiano. Opposite the palace is the **church of San Gaetano**. Originally a Romanesque structure, it was entirely rebuilt in the Florentine Baroque style by Matteo Nigetti, Gherardo and Pier Francesco Silvani. The aisleless interior is lined in black marble. In the second chapel on the left is the *Martyrdom of St. Laurence* painted by Pietro da Cortona.

Via Tornabuoni — This is the most aristocratic street in Florence and one of the most beautiful in the world. Lovely old palaces, fine shops, and smart restaurants are visible along both sides of the street. On the right, at Number 19 is **Palazzo Larderel**, a lovely late Renaissance building designed by Giovanni Antonio Dosio (1580). Opposite, at number 2, is **Palazzo Corsi**. It was restructured in 1875, although the original construction was designed by Michelozzo whose elegant inner courtyard is still extant. **Palazzo Viviani**, formerly **Palazzo della Robbia** (number 15), was originally the home of the renowned della Robbia family. It was restructured in 1639 by G.B. Foggini. At this point Via Tornabuoni intersects, on the left, with Via Strozzi, a busy street leading into Piazza della Repubblica, while, on our right, two streets, Via della Spada and Via della Vigna Nuova, branch out in the opposite direction. Midway along Via della Vigna Nuova, is the **Loggia dei Rucellai** designed by Leon Battista Alberti and built in 1468. The loggia was the setting for the joyous and not so joyous celebrations of the aristocratic Rucellai family. Opposite, at number 18, is **Palazzo Rucellai**, one of the landmarks of Early Renaissance architecture. The building was built by Bernardo Rossellino, but the design, of revolutionary importance to 15th century civilian architecture, was Leon Battista Alberti's (1446-1451). The three storey building is faced with smooth rusticated stone blocks, cornices and pilaster strips with harmoniously spaced twin-arched mullioned windows. Those interested may ring for the custodian who will open up the restored **Rucellai Chapel** (around the corner on Via della Spada). Inside is an altarpiece shaped like a temple, called the

123

Palazzo Strozzi.

Edicola del Santo Sepolcro, which Leon Battista Alberti created in colored marble for Giovanni di Paolo Ruccellai.

Retracing ones steps, one returns to Via Tornabuoni, to be confronted by majestic Palazzo Strozzi.

STROZZI PALACE

Filippo Strozzi, a Florentine merchant of long-standing wealth (he had the merit of introducing into Tuscany not only the cultivation of artichokes, but also a good variety of fig), commissioned Benedetto da Maiano to build the palace in 1489; Benedetto was succeeded by Cronaca who directed the work until 1504. Later the construction was interrupted and resumed several times: the Strozzi family fell into disfavour in 1538, the palace was confiscated by Cosimo I dei Medici and given back 30 years later. Now it houses the **Gabinetto Vieusseux** and other cultural organisations; exhibitions are held here as well as the *Biennial Antiques Exhibition Fair*.

The massive building has a stone plinth all round it at the base, projecting like a bench; the exterior recalls that of Palazzo Medici-Riccardi, with pronounced

Palazzo Spini-Ferroni with the Column of Justice in the foreground.

rustication; at the top is a magnificent cornice by Cronaca; the two upper storeys have fine mullioned, twin-arched windows: The wrought-iron corner lanterns, torch brackets and ring which add handsome decorative touches to the façade are by Nicolò Grosso known as *"il Caparra"*.

Continuing down Via Tornabuoni, on the left, is **Palazzo Altoviti** surmounted by a loggia. It was joined to **Palazzo Sangalletti** by a 19th century architect, Silvestri (in 1827). To the right is **Palazzo Giacomini** designed by Gherardo Silvani (17th century) at number 5. Next to it, at number 3, is the 14th century **Palazzo Minerbetti**. The street continues thus briefly, crowded with elegant, fashionable shops, until it widens out into Piazza Santa Trinita.

PIAZZA SANTA TRINITA

Surrounded by noble mansions, the square is at the beginning of Via Tornabuoni, with the **Column of Justice** in the centre. It came from the Baths of Caracalla in Rome and supports the statue of *Justice* by Francesco del Tadda (1581). The fine large battlemented palace that extends as far as Lungarno Acciaioli is the 13th century **Palazzo Spini-Ferroni** (restored in the 19th century); at No. 1 of the piazza is **Palazzo Bartolini-Salimbeni**, Baccio d'Agnolo's masterpiece, with its unusual stone-cross partitioned windows (1517-20). Baccio d'Agnolo (1520-1529), was soundly criticized for his great daring in inventing new architectural motifs. He responded by having a Latin inscription engraved on the architrave to the effect that it is easier to criticize something than to imitate it (*"carpere promptius quam imitari"*). The western side of the square is occupied by the church of Santa Trinita.

Borgo Santi Apostoli, right off Piazza Santa Trinita, is one of the most charming medieval streets in Florence. The towerhouses and palaces along it all date from the 13th and 14th centuries. The restored 11th century **church of Santi Apostoli** is set back on a tiny square midway down the street. The 16th century portal cut into its striking Romanesque façade is a fine work attributed to Benedetto da Rovezzano. The interior has retained its original structure. Above the sacristy door (to the right of the choir) is *the tomb of Bindo Altoviti* surmounted by a statue of *Charity*, attributed to Ammannati. To the left of the main altar is a glazed terracotta *tabernacle* by Andrea della Robbia, and the *tomb of Oddo Altoviti* by Benedetto da Rovezzano (1508). Here too, is the flint for lighting the sacred fire on Easter Day which according to tradition was brought from the Holy Land by Crusader Pazzino de' Pazzi.

SANTA TRINITA

The church was built by the Vallombrosan monastic order in the 11th century, although Niccolò Pisano restructured it in the 13th century and it was thereafter enlarged. The Baroque façade was designed by Buontalenti in 1594. The statue of St. Alexis on the left and the bas-relief depicting the Trinity above the central doorway are by Giovanni Caccini.

THE INTERIOR – This important Gothic church contains equally important works of art of the 14th and 15th centuries. The side chapels were added on in the 14th century. Upon the inner façade you can see the remains of the original Gothic church structure. Right aisle: on the altar of the third chapel *Virgin and Child with Saints* by Neri di Bicci. The fourth chapel was painted by Lorenzo Monaco and has Fra Angelico's *scenes from the life of Mary* and *Prophets* on the ceiling. On the altar is a panel painting of the *Annunciation*. In the fifth chapel is a marble altar by Benedetto da Rovezzano. In the right transept, next to the Sacristy where we find the *tomb of Onofrio Strozzi* by Pietro di Niccolò Lamberti (1421), we encounter the second right transept *Sassetti Chapel* with its famous *fresco cycle* by Domenico Ghirlandaio (1483-1486). Outside, above the arch is a fresco showing a statue of David on a column. On the right side is the *Tiberine Sibyl foretelling the birth of Christ to Augustus*. Inside there are four *sibyls* frescoed on the ceiling and scenes from the life of *St. Francis*. Starting from the upper left: 1) *St. Francis giving up his earthly possessions*, 2) *approval of the Franciscan Rule*, and 3) *the trial by fire before the Sultan*. The lower register starting from the left shows: 4) *St. Francis receiving the Stigmata*, to the right, 5) *the death of St. Francis*; on the wall behind the altar: 6) *St. Francis, invoked after his death, resuscitates a young man of the Spini family*. Below are portraits of Francesco Sassetti and his wife, Nera Corsi, who commissioned the work. One of Ghirlandaio's best-loved works, the *Adoration of the Shepherds* (1495), is on the altar. The *tombs of Francesco and Nera Sassetti* attributed to Giuliano da Sangallo (1491) are in the niches either side of the altar. In the adjoining chapel is

126

The church of Santa Trinita.

a huge *Crucifix*. It is known as the "Crucifix of St. Giovanni Gualberto" since the painted Christ reputedly nodded his head in approval when Giovanni knelt before it after having forgiven the man who had murdered his brother. On the altar of the main chapel is an altarpiece with the *Holy Trinity* and *Saints* by Mariotto di Nardo (1416). The frescoes by Alessio Baldovinetti (c. 1471) on the ceiling are unfortunately in very poor condition. In the left transept in the second chapel to the left of the main one, is an exquisite marble carving by Luca della Robbia: the *tomb of Benozzo Federighi, Bishop of Fiesole*. On the walls are frescoes with *scenes from the life of St. Bartholomew* by Giovanni da Ponte. In the second front chapel is a 15th century Florentine school painting of *Christ's encounter with Mary on the way to Calvary*. In the fourth chapel is a 15th century Sienese school altarpiece with the *Coronation of the Virgin*. A stone plaque indicates the *tomb of Dino Compagni* (1250-1324), Dante's friend and chronicler of his times. The third chapel contains a panel painting by Neri di Bicci of the *Annunciation*, above the altar. The walls are frescoed with the *Disputation of St. Catherine* by followers of Giotto. The Roman Sarcophagus with a reclining figure is the *tomb of Giuliano Davanzati*. On the altar of the second chapel is the *Mystic Marriage of St. Catherine* by Antonio del Ceraiolo (16th century); frescoes by Ridolfo del Ghirlandaio of *St. Jerome* and the *Annunciation* (1503) are painted on the walls.

127

The bridge of the Holy Trinity (Ponte a Santa Trinita).

PONTE SANTA TRINITA

Leaving Ponte Vecchio aside, this is certainly the most beautiful and stately bridge in Florence. It was originally built in wood in 1252 and was destroyed and rebuilt several times over the years until it was given its splendid Renaissance lines by Bartolommeo Ammannati in 1567-70. It has three slender arches supported by powerful piers, while the statues of the four Seasons that decorate each of the four corner plinths of the bridge were added in 1608. It was mined during the last World War and was blown up on the 4th August 1944. It was reconstructed after the war exactly as it had been and where it had been previously, by the architects Brizzi and Gizdulich who used all the original stones they had managed to recover, including the statues.

Lungarno Corsini – This is one of the most attractive stretches along the right bank of the river. It was named after the Corsini, a family numbering several illustrious historical figures among their ancestors–two of these are Lorenzo Corsini (Pope Clement XII, 13th century) and Andrea Corsini, Bishop of Fiesole. Aristocratic mansions are built all along the river. At number 2 is Palazzo Gianfigliazzi (where the British Consulate is located) which was restructured in the 19th century along with the adjoining building, also the property of the Gianfigliazzi. Number 10 is **Palazzo Corsini** built by P. F. Silvani and A. Ferri (1648-1656). One of the outstanding examples of Florentine Baroque, the palace

Ponte a Santa Trinita — The figures of Autumn and Winter, two of the four
statues placed at the ends of the bridge.

consists of a main section flanked by wings, on top of which is a terrace
decorated with statuary. At the far end of the courtyard on the left is a great spiral
staircase designed by Silvani and on the right a monumental one designed by
Ferri and decorated with several antique statues, including one of Clement XII. On
the second floor is a fine little art museum, **Galleria Corsini**. The collection,
started by Lorenzo Corsini in 1765, in one of the most outstanding private
collections in Italy. There are works by Raphael, Filippino Lippi, Andrea del
Castagno, Botticelli, Signorelli, Caravaggio, Andrea del Sarto, as well as 17th and
18th century Italian and foreign masters.

Lungarno Corsini ends at the bridge known as **Ponte alla Carraia** (rebuilt) at
Piazza Goldoni. If one proceeds along the river one reaches Lungarno Amerigo
Vespucci which runs into Piazza Ognissanti. Going on even further, and
meanwhile enjoying the lovely view on the other side of the river (the dome of the
church of San Frediano with Monte Oliveto in the background, and the San
Miniato hill on the left), one soon comes to the **Amerigo Vespucci bridge**. The
bridge was named after the great explorer who discovered Brazil and whose name
was given to North and South America. Built in 1957, the bridge was designed by
Enzo Gori, Giuseppe Gori, Ernesto Nelli, and Riccardo Morandi. The *"lungarno"*
ends at the reconstructed **Ponte della Vittoria** on the left and a huge landscaped
square to the right. The square, Piazza Vittorio Veneto, is arranged around an
equestrian statue of King Vittorio Emanuele II by Emilio Zocchi (1890).

The Cascine Park — The largest park in Florence and one of the most extensive
in Italy. It starts from Piazza Vittorio Veneto and stretches for over 3 kms. along
the river Arno's right bank. It derives its name from a number of farmhouses
(cascine) that belonged to the Medici and to the Hapsburgh-Lorraine families in

Equestrian monument of Victor Emanuel II, by Emilio Zocchi, in the centre of Piazza Vittorio Veneto.

this area. It was opened to the public towards the middle of the 17th century and has since been one of the Florentines' favourite haunts, specially on feast-days and popular occasions (the famous "Festa del Grillo" - Feast of the Cricket is held here on Ascension Day). The Faculty of Husbandry or Agricultural Sciences, as well as the Training Institute for Airforce cadets, playing fields, two race-courses are all within the precincts of the Cascine Park. At the end of the park is the *Monument to the Indian*: a little domed pagoda-like pavillion which shelters a bronze bust of Rajaram Cuttraputti, Maharajah of Kolepoor, who died aged twenty in Florence, in 1870 and was cremated here, in accordance with the Hindu rite which demands that such a site be at the meeting point of two rivers (in this case the Arno and the Mugnone).

OGNISSANTI

The church faces onto the square named after it, flanked by large hotel buildings. There is a bronze group by Romanelli in the centre of the square of *Hercules wrestling with a lion.* The graceful Baroque façade of the church (1637) was designed by Matteo Nigetti, whereas the belltower dates back to the 15th century, The glazed terracotta relief in the lunette above the doorway of the church showing the *Coronation of the Virgin*, is by Benedetto Buglioni.

THE INTERIOR – The aisless interior contains some great works of art such as Domenico Ghirlandaio's fresco (second altar on the right) of the *Vespucci family sheltered beneath the Virgin's cloak* (c. 1470). The youth dressed in red between the Virgin and the old man is Amerigo Vespucci himself. Between the third and fourth altars is a fresco of *St. Augustine in his study* by Botticelli. In a chapel of the right transept is a small disk which marks the spot where Botticelli is buried.

The church of Ognissanti (All Saints) overlooking its crowded square.

The frescoes in the dome and four pendentives of the main chapel are by Giovanni da San Giovanni (1617). Opposite Botticelli's fresco of St. Augustine is one of *St. Jerome in his study* by Ghirlandaio (1480). From the left side of church we enter the lovely Renaissance cloister with frescoed lunettes by Giovanni da San Giovanni (1616-1619) and Jacopo Ligozzi (1625). The subject of the frescoes is the *life of St. Francis*. From the cloister we enter the refectory. On the far wall is Ghirlandaio's renowned *Last Supper* fresco (1480). It is said that Leonardo da Vinci drew his inspiration for his own version of the scene (in the Dominican monastery adjoining the church of Santa Maria delle Grazie in Milan) from Ghirlandaio's masterpiece.

After continuing down Borgo Ognissanti, we turn left into Via dei Fossi which leads right into Piazza Santa Maria Novella.

PIAZZA SANTA MARIA NOVELLA

This is one of the most beautiful squares in the city with its lovely 15th century arcade, the **Loggia of San Paolo**, and opposite it, the striking façade of the church of Santa Maria Novella. The loggia is adorned with glazed terracotta medallions by Giovanni della Robbia and a fine lunette with *St. Francis greeting St. Dominic* by Andrea della Robbia beneath the arcade. The two marble *obelisks* in the middle of the square are by Giambologna (1608). Surmounted by bronze fleurs-de-lys and resting upon bronze tortoises, these columns once served as the pivots (or end posts) around which the chariot races which Cosimo I, inspired by Roman chariot contests, instituted in 1563 used to turn, when charging around the track, laid out in the square.

131

The church of Santa Maria Novella overlooking its sunny square.

SANTA MARIA NOVELLA

The great Dominican church is one of the most renowned in Florence. It was built, in 1246 on the site of a pre-existing oratory by two friars of the order: Fra Sisto and Fra Ristoro. The construction of the nave and side-aisles started in 1279, whilst the façade was commenced in the 14th century, the lower section of it being completed by the middle of the century in the typically Florentine Romanesque-Gothic style. The belltower and the sacristy were finished by 1360 by another Dominican friar: Jacopo Talenti. After the middle of the 15th century, Leon Battista Alberti completed the central doorway and the upper section of the façade, with a rose window, architraved tympanum and lateral volutes in lovely white and green marble patterns of refined elegance. The garden laid out along the right side of the church, is the ancient cemetery of Plaona, and is surrounded by tombs sheltered within Gothic arched niches, called "avelli" (tombs).

INTERIOR — The Cistercian influence is clearly apparent, albeit a softer, Italian version of it. There are two wide aisles flanking the great nave and multi-columned piers sweep up to support ogival arched cross-vaults. The extremely long nave is broken by a hundred meter long presbitery, but thanks to the artifice of reducing the spaces between the piers the nearer they get to the

Santa Maria Novella — Interior.

apse, the impression of depth, which strikes one upon entering the church, is accentuated. The altars along the aisles are by Vasari (1565-1571). Right aisle: in the second bay is the *Monument of the Blessed Villana dei Cerchi* by Bernardo Rossellino (1451). Just beyond the fifth bay is the entrance to the **Cappella della Pura** (1474). The *wooden crucifix* on the altar is painted with scenes of the life of Christ (early 14th century). The door on the right leads to the old cemetery with several wall tombs and coats-of-arms. Right transept: on the right, is a *shrine with a bust of St. Antoninus* (15th century). High up is the Gothic *tomb of Tedice Aliotti, Bishop of Fiesole* (d. 1336), by Tino di Camaino. On the left is the *tomb of Aldobrando Cavalcanti, Bishop of Orvieto* by Nino Pisano. Below it is the *tomb of Joseph, Patriarch of Constantinople* who died in Florence in 1439. The staircase at the end of the transept leads up to the **Cappella Rucellai** where Duccio's famous *Virgin enthroned* of c. 1285 (now one of the Uffizi's treasures) originally hung. On the walls are remains of 14th century frescoes depicting the *Martyrdom of St.*

133

Santa Maria Novella — The Crowning of the Virgin: stained glass rose-window designed by Andrea di Bonaiuto or da Firenze.

Catherine. On the far wall of the transept is the **Capella Bardi** with remains of frescoes by followers of Giotto (14th century). On the pillar to the right of the entrance is a 13th century relief of *St. George in the act of blessing*. On the right is a twin-arched mullioned window dating from the original 13th century building. Next we come to the **Cappella Filippo Strozzi** frescoed by Filippino Lippi (1503) with *Scenes from the lives of the apostles Philip and John*. This is one of the master's last works. The figures on the ceiling are Adam, Noah, Abraham, and Jacob. Behind the altar is the fine carved *tomb of Filippo Strozzi* by Benedetto da Maiano (1491-1493). **Main Chapel**: the bronze *tomb slab of Leonardo Dati* by Lorenzo Ghiberti (1423) is in front of the steps leading up to the altar. To the right of the altar is a lovely candlestick shaped like a twining column, for the Easter candle by Pier Giovanni Tedesco (14th century). Its companion is a copy. On the modern altar is a bronze *crucifix*, by Giambologna. Apse: the wooden choir fittings and lectern by Baccio d'Agnolo were modified by Vasari. In the chapel is the renowned fresco cycle on the *life of the Virgin and St. John the Baptist* painted by Ghirlandaio whose helpers included a talented young artist, Michelangelo (1485-1490). The figures are portraits of members of the Tornabuoni family who commissioned the work and friends of theirs, making the frescoes a valuable chronicle of 15th century Florentine life. On the ceiling are the four Evangelists. The Life of Mary on the left wall starting from below is depicted as

134

Santa Maria Novella - Birth of the Virgin, by Girlandaio (detail).

follows: 1) *Joachim expelled from the Temple because of his childless state*, 2) *Birth of the Virgin*, 3) *Presentation of the Virgin at the Temple*, 4) *Espousal of the Virgin*, 5) *Adoration of the Magi*, 6) *Slaughter of the Innocents* and, in the lunette, *Death and Assumption of the Virgin*. Far wall, in the lunette, *Coronation of the Virgin* on either side of the window, *St. Dominic burning heretical books*, *Death of St. Peter the Martyr*, the *Annunciation*, *St. John in the desert*. Below, the praying figures are portraits of Francesco Tornabuoni and his wife Francesca Pitti, the sponsors. On the opposite wall starting from the lower righthand side is the life of the Baptist: *the Angel appearing to Zacharias, the Birth of the Baptist, Zacharias writing his son's name, the Baptist preaching, the Baptism of Christ*, and in the lunette, *Herod's feast*. Left transept: **Cappella Gondi** with remains of 13th century frescoes by Greek artists and a painted wooden *crucifix* by Filippino Brunelleschi. The crucifix has been called "Christ of the eggs" due to the fact that Donatello (who had carved a crucifix criticized by Brunelleschi now in the church of Santa Croce) was so struck by its beauty, when he first saw it, that he dropped the eggs he was holding. Next is the **Cappella Gaddi** with stuccoes and ceiling frescoes by Alessandro Allori. On the altar is a painting of *Christ resuscitating a young girl* by Bronzino. Passing to the left side of the transept we climb a few steps to the **Cappella Strozzi** with frescoes by Nardo di Cione (c. 1357) depicting the *Last Judgment*, in the middle, *Hell*, on the right, and *Paradise*, on the left, inspired by Dante's *Divine Comedy*. In the Paradise scene is a portrait of Dante who died in 1321, just a few years before the frescoes were painted. From this side we enter the **sacristy** designed by Jacopo Talenti (1350). Of note are a glazed *terracotta washstand* by Giovanni della Robbia (1498) and two *Crucifixions*, one attributed to Giotto and one to Maso di Bartolomeo. Left aisle: along the wall is one of Masaccio's last and greatest works, the fresco of the *Holy Trinity* (c. 1428) with its unusual perspective view.

135

Santa Maria Novella — The Holy Trinity, frescoed by Masaccio and detail of Ghirlandaio's frescoes.

The Cloisters of Santa Maria Novella — Access is through the baroque gateway to the left of the façade of the church. Turning right, the first cloister one comes to is the **Green Cloister**, constructed after 1350, in which late-Romanesque trends are still apparent. It derives its name from the frescoes in green pigment which decorate three sides of the colonnade, and were painted by several 15th century painters including Paolo Uccello, who depicted the Episodes from the Genesis (see the magnificent *Flood* in one of the lunettes). From one side of the cloister, one enters the *Great Chapel of the Spaniards* (Cappellone degli Spagnoli), which was built in the 14th century by Francesco Talenti as a Chapter House and was used by Eleonora of Toledo's Spanish Household in the 16th century (Eleonora was Cosimo Ist's wife). The walls of the Chapel are entirely covered with frescoes by Andrea di Bonaiuto, a Florentine artist, active in the second half of the 14th century and much influenced by the Sienese Gothic school. The theme of the frescoes is the Rule of the Order of St. Dominic and St. Thomas Aquinas. Right: a magnificent rendition of the *Church Militant*; left: *Apotheosis of St. Thomas Aquinas*; entrance wall: *Episodes from the Life of St. Peter*; wall opposite the entrance and ceiling vault: *Scenes from the New Testament*. Behind the Great Chapel of the Spaniards, one proceeds along a corridor and reaches the **Little Cloister of the Dead** (Chiostrino dei Morti), where one encounters the *Funerary Chapel of the Strozzi family*, with frescoes by Orcagna. At the end of the cloister, there is a small chapel, with a *Resurrection*, attributed to Nardo di Cione and a *Noli me tangere*, in enamelled coloured terracotta, by the Della Robbia workshop. One proceeds hence to the **Great Cloister** (Chiostro Grande) which is decorated all the way around by excellent 15th and 16th century Tuscan artists; there are over fifty arches and is one of the most magnificent in Florence.

FIFTH ITINERARY

Piazza del Duomo — Via Cavour — Refectory of St. Apollonia — Scalzo Cloister — Piazza San Marco (Church of San Marco; San Marco or Fra Angelico Museum) — Academy Gallery and the Tribuna of the David — Piazza Santissima Annunziata (Church of Santissima Annunziata; Hospital of the Innocents; Archeological Museum) — Synagogue — Cloister of Santa Maria Maddalena de' Pazzi — Church of Sant'Ambrogio.

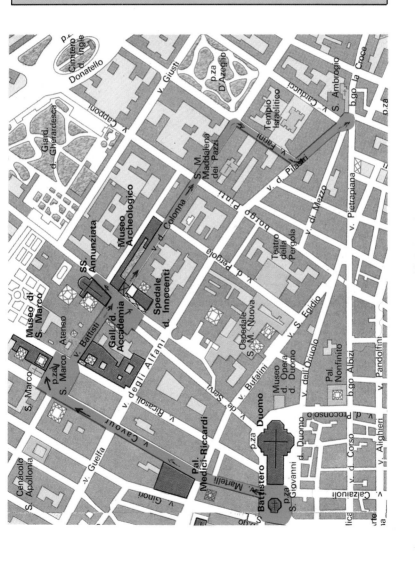

Via Cavour – From Piazza del Duomo, one proceeds along Via Martelli, which becomes Via Cavour, flanked by severe-looking 17th and 18th century mansions which lend the street a very imposing appearance. On ones left, one encounters **Palazzo Medici-Riccardi** (see first itinerary). Further on, where Via Cavour drives laterally through Piazza San Marco, one finds Via degli Arazzieri to ones left, which becomes Via XXVII Aprile, Nr. 1 of which street is the **Refectory of St. Apollonia**. It was the refectory of a Benedictine convent and contains the frescoes painted there by Andrea del Castagno in 1450. The intensely realistic *Last Supper* is one of the most significant works of the artist. On the left wall: a *Crucifixion*, a *Deposition* and a *Resurrection*; in the lunettes: a *Crucifixion*, *Saints* and a *Lamentation over the dead Christ*. Continuing along Via Cavour, one encounters a great palace at Nr. 63, which is now the Court of Appeal, whereas the **"Scalzo Cloister"** is a little further on at Nr. 69. The name "Scalzo" (barefoot) indicates the barefoot bearer of the Cross of the religious confraternity, which was founded in 1376 who used to walk in the processions through the streets of the town. The little inner 16th century cloister is frescoed all around with 16 chiaroscuro *Scenes from the Life of St. John the Baptist* (1514-1526) nearly all painted by Andrea del Sarto – two being by Franciabigio.

PIAZZA SAN MARCO

A monument to *General Manfredo Fanti*, by Pio Fedi (1837) stands in the centre of the gardens in the middle of the square. The buidings on the square include the church of San Marco and its adjacent monastery (which is also the Fra Angelico Museum), the headquarters of the University of Florence, and at the corner of Via Ricasoli, the **Academy of Fine Arts** (you can see its 14th century porch), once housed in the Hospital of St. Matthew.

The Academy Museum (where Michelangelo's original David may be viewed) is at Via Ricasoli 60.

SAN MARCO

Although it was originally built at the end of the 13th century in Romanesque-Gothic style, it was rebuilt when Cosimo the Elder commissioned Michelozzo to restructure it for the Dominican friars in 1452. Transformed once more by Giambologna in 1580, it was not until 1678 that Pier Francesco Silvani, making even greater changes, gave it its present appearance. The Baroque façade was designed by a monk, Fra Gioacchino Pronti, in 1780, although the wooden main doorway was already in place during the lifetime of the famous Dominican monk, Savonarola (1490s). In fact, we know it withstood an attempt made to set it on fire when a revolt broke out – enraged citizens trying to get into the church so that they could capture and kill Savonarola.

THE INTERIOR – The painting on the lovely carved ceiling of the aisleless church depicts the *Virgin in Glory* (by G. Antonio Pucci, 1725). Above the entrance is a huge *crucifix* by followers of Giotto (14th century). At the first altar on the

San Marco — Interior.

righthand side is *St. Thomas of Aquinas* by Santi di Tito, at the second *Virgin and saints* by Fra Bartolomeo (1509), at the third a huge 8th century mosaic of the *Virgin in prayer* (it originally belonged to Pope John VII's oratory), and, at the fourth, framed by an arch surmounted by a statue of *St. Zenobius* by Giambologna (1580), the *Virgin with an image of St. Dominic* by Matteo Rosselli. At the end of the nave a Baroque door leads to the vestibule and **Sacristy** designed by Michelozzo (1437-1443), where one finds a reclining statue of *St. Antoninus* designed by Giambologna and executed by Portinari. To the left of the **Main Chapel** is another chapel, the **Serragli or Sacrament** decorated with frescoes by Santi di Tito and Passignano. Next comes the **Salviati or St. Antoninus Chapel**, designed by Giambologna and built between 1580 and 1589. The subject of the fine frescoes by Passignano is the *Burial of St. Antoninus*. The bronze and marble decoration is also by Giambologna and Pietro Francavilla, one of his pupils. The wall tombs of two of the best-known humanists, *Pico della Mirandola* and *Poliziano*, are along the left wall of the church.

MUSEUM OF SAN MARCO

The entrance to the museum is to the right of the church. The museum was originally a monastery, first belonging to the Vallombrosan and later to the Silvestrini orders. In the 1430s Cosimo the Elder commissioned Michelozzo to restructure the whole building. By the time Michelozzo started work on the project (1437-1457), the monastery had been turned over to the Dominicans, the order of Fra Angelico. The painter-friar lived

139

Museum of San Marco — Deposition from the Cross, by Fra Angelico.

here between 1435 to 1445. Other famous men as well lived in San Marco: Girolamo Savonarola (1489-1498), St. Antoninus Pierozzi, Archbishop of Florence, and Fra Bartolomeo, another great Renaissance painter-friar. When the monastery was suppressed in 1866, it was turned into a state museum, chiefly designed to house the Fra Angelico paintings formerly dispersed amongst the Florentine museums and churches.

THE CLOISTER OF ST. ANTONINUS — A typical example of Renaissance monastic architecture, the cloister is decorated with 16th-17th century frescoes of scenes from the life of St. Antoninus. Of particular note is the lunette fresco (near the *Hospice* entrance) by Bernardino Poccetti showing the original façade of the Cathedral of Florence designed by Arnolfo di Cambio. Several frescoes by Fra Angelico are to be found here: *St. Peter the Martyr* (far end, left, in the lunette above the door), *St. Dominic at the foot of the Cross* (on the wall opposite the entrance) *Lamentation over the dead Christ* (at the end of the same wall, above the door) and *Christ clad as a pilgrim received by the Dominican monks* (above the doorway on the next wall).

OSPIZIO DEI PELLEGRINI (Pilgrim's Hospice) — This is the world's foremost collection of paintings by the mystic monk and artist, Fra Angelico, who reputedly could not paint a Crucifixion without weeping. It is divided into three sections. In the first section is the renowned *Linen merchants Altarpiece* which depicts the

Museum of San Marco — Madonna and Child with Saints, by Fra Angelico.

Virgin enthroned and *music-making angels* (1433); the lovely marble frame was designed by Ghiberti. In addition, there are several other remarkable panels such as the *Marriage* and *Death of the Virgin, Zacharias writing his son's name*, two versions of the *Virgin enthroned*, and the *Miracle and burial of Sts. Cosmas and Damian*. The second section contains thirty-five panels with *scenes from the life of Christ* (1450). They used to decorate the cupboard of the treasure of the church of Santissima Annunziata. The *Flight into Egypt, Nativity*, and *Christ entering Jerusalem* panels are by Angelico's own hand, whereas the rest were painted with the help of other artists except for three by Alessio Baldovinetti. The outstanding works in the third section include the *Virgin of the Star*, the *Last Judgment*, the *Coronation of the Virgin*, the *Deposition*, the *Annunciation*, and the *Adoration of the Magi*.

SALA DEL LAVABO (The Basin Room) — The basin is by the della Robbia workshop. Among the 16th century paintings decorating the walls is an interesting chiaroscuro *Virgin and saints* by Fra Bartolomeo.

THE MAIN REFECTORY — The room is hung with works by Fra Bartolomeo, including his fine *Last Judgement*. The huge fresco showing *St. Dominic's miraculous supper* was painted by Giovanni Antonio Sogliani (1536).

THE CHAPTER ROOM — Opposite the entrance is a Fra Angelico fresco of the *Crucifixion with various saints and the founders of the religious orders*, a superb

Museum of San Marco – Annunciation and Noli me tangere, both frescoed in the monks' cells, by Fra Angelico.

blend of dramatic effect and refined pictorial style. On the left wall is a tempera on canvas of *St. Antoninus in adoration* by Baldovinetti (16th century) and opposite, a painted wooden *crucifix* by Baccio da Montelupo (1500).

FIRST FLOOR – At the top of the stairs are frescoes of the *Annunciation* and *St. Dominic adoring the Cross*, two marvellous examples of Fra Angelico's mystical imagery. On either side of the corridors are little cubicles, once the cells inhabited by the Dominican monks. Each one contains a fresco, either by Fra Angelico himself or by his pupils who worked from his designs. The outstanding frescoes are: *Noli me tangere* (cell 1), the *Annunciation* (cell 3), the *Crucifixion* (cell 4), the *Transfiguration* (cell 6), the *Mocking of Christ* (cell 7), the *Coronation of the Virgin* (cell 9), and the *Virgin and Child with Saints* (cell 11). At the end of the corridor we come to the **Quartiere del Priore** (Prior's Apartments), a three-roomed apartment, in which Fra Girolamo Savonarola, the reformer monk, lived until April 8, 1498 when he was taken prisoner to be tried for heresy. In the first cell, the vestibule, are two paintings of Savonarola being burned at the stake on May 3, 1498, by painters of the period. There are also two *portraits* by Fra Bartolomeo, one of *Savonarola* and one of *St. Peter Martyr*. In the second cell (study) is a wooden *crucifix* by Baccio da Montelupo that belonged to Savonarola. The bibles on the desk as well as the chalices, cowl, tunic, and rosary beads in the cabinet all once belonged to the monk. In the third cell (bedroom) is a silk processional standard with a *Crucifixion* painted in the style of Fra Angelico. Retracing our steps, we can stop at the cells along the left side frescoed with crucifixions by pupils of Fra Angelico. Cell 31 was once inhabited by St. Antoninus. The frescoes in the entrance and cells 34 (*Christ praying in the garden*) and 35 (*Communion of the Apostles*) by Fra Angelico's helpers, are particularly worthy of note. At the end of the righthand corridor are two cells, 38 and 39, which were used by Cosimo the Elder when he joined the community to pray and meditate.

Museum of San Marco — The Library with its precious illuminated codexes.

THE LIBRARY — This lovely Renaissance hall with its graceful Ionic columns was designed by Michelozzo (1441). The showcases contain precious 14th-15th century manuscripts, many of which are illuminated.

THE REFECTORY — Returning to the ground floor we enter the refectory decorated with a fresco of the *Last Supper* by Ghirlandaio. It greatly resembles the fresco on the same subject he painted in the refectory of Ognissanti.

THE CLOISTER OF SAN DOMENICO — It too was designed by Michelozzo. Along the arcades and in the adjoining rooms are fragments from the medieval buildings in the old center of Florence torn down in the 19th century.

ACADEMY GALLERY

This is one of the most famous galleries in Italy, visited by thousands of people, chiefly thanks to the fact that the original statue of the **David** as well as other famous sculptures by Michelangelo are displayed in this museum. The Gallery, (Via Ricasoli 60, near Piazza San Marco) was founded in 1784 by Grand Duke Peter Leopold of Hapsburg-Lorraine, as an Academy of Fine Arts with the object of housing all the schools of art, drawing and sculpture already existing in the city under a single roof; the gallery was thus created with the specific purpose of helping the pupils to know and study the Old Masters. Many of the works hung here at the disposal of the students came from a previous collection, that belonged to the Academy of the Art of Drawing, an institution of great prestige, founded in 1562 by Cosimo I, which was attended by all the greatest artists of the time, and was an updated version of the 14th century Company of Painters of St. Luke. The already considerable collection of paintings was increased as a result of the suppression of churches and monasteries (1786 and 1808); there were further acquisitions and in 1873 the *David* was brought here, followed in 1911 by the *Prisoners* and *St. Matthew*, while the *Pietà* only arrived in 1940, when it was bought by the State.

ROOM OF THE COLOSSUS — The entrance is through the vestibule where the ticket counter has been set up. The works displayed are 16th century paintings,

The Academy Gallery — The Madonna of the Girdle with Saints Thomas and Michael, by Granacci and Deposition from the Cross, by Filippino Lippi and Pietro Perugino; *below*: the David «Tribuna» Hall.

The Academy Gallery — Two of the four «Prisoners» by Michelangelo in the «Tribuna» Hall.

including several by Francesco Granacci, the *Annunciation* and other paintings by Mariotto Albertinelli, *St. John the Baptist* and *Mary Magdalen* by Filippino Lippi, a fine *Deposition* by Lippi and Perugino, a *Virgin and saints* by Perugino, a *Virgin and Child with saints* by Ghirlandaio, as well as others by Fra Bartolomeo and Francesco Botticini. The sculpture in the middle is Giambologna's plaster model for his marble group of the *Rape of the Sabine Women*.

THE HALL AND THE "TRIBUNA" — The "Tribuna" was built in 1882 by Emilio de Fabris, the architect who designed the façade of the Cathedral, to house the David by Michelangelo, which had been transferred to the museum a few years earlier. The "Tribuna", like a large apse, is at the end of a hall, along the sides of which are other sculptures by Michelangelo: the *Prisoners, St. Matthew* and the *Palestrina Pietà*. The **Prisoners** formed part of the project for the tomb of Pope Julius II which was to stand in the Basilica of St. Peter's in Rome. The monument was commissioned by Julius II himself in 1505 but after incredible vicissitudes a much reduced tomb was placed forty years later, in the Roman church of San Pietro in Vincoli, where there is also the famous statue of Moses. The dramatic unfinished figures seem to be striving to free themselves from the oppression of the marble. Another splendid work by Michelangelo is the **St. Matthew** sculptured perhaps in 1504; it is one of the first example of Michelangelo's so-called "unfinished" style, that is the crude result of chiselling, without any finishing off; an expressive, violent way of letting us glimpse absolute, incomparable beauty that only the mind can perceive. Even more tormented, as if torn by desperate religious anguish, is the **Palestrina Pietà**, one of the master's last works. Despite the quality of this sculpture, some critics disagree with its attribution to Michelangelo because it is not mentioned by any historical source. The **David** was carved between 1501 and April 1504, and was finished a month

The Academy Gallery — Michelangelo's David.

after the sculptor's 29th birthday. In June the same year, 1502, the splendid work, already much admired, was placed, upon the decision of a committee of distinguished artists, on the steps of Palazzo Vecchio, as if to symbolise and defend republican liberty. David, a handsome fully grown man, and not the boy described in the Bible, was taken as a symbol of the two civic virtues of Strength, with his harmonious but powerful body (static on the right side, with the hand clutching the stone, while the left leg is pressed forward and the arm bends with the sling) and Resolution, in the watchful, resolute face, like an idealised Hercules. In 1527, during an uprising, the left arm of the statue was broken off by

147

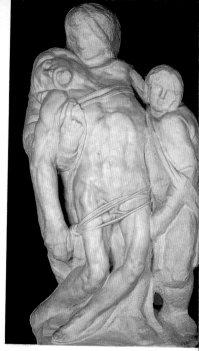

The Academy Gallery — St. Matthew and the Deposition or Pietà, both by Michelangelo; *opposite*: Madonna and Child with angels, by Sandro Botticelli.

a bench flung from the palace. Vasari recovered the fragments and the restoration was carried out in 1543. In 1873 the David was taken to the Accademia and replaced on the steps by a copy. The gigantic proportions (the statue alone, without the base, is over 13 feet high), its dramatic tension, the proud, beautiful face, confidently sizing up his adversary, the precision of the anatomy, with muscles tensed for action, the superb moral and human dignity of the personality, all express the youthful vision of Michelangelo, who endows the biblical champion with a veritably Renaissance-like heroic quality. Upon the walls of the David "Tribuna", a number of paintings by Florentine artists of Michelangelo's circle replace the series of 16th century Flemish tapestries illustrating the Stories of Adam and Eve, such as for instance: paintings by Pontormo, Alessandro Allori, Granacci, Santi di Tito, etc.

THE FLORENTINE ROOMS — I — Access to these rooms is from the Hall of the Prisoners. The paintings exhibited here are by early Renaissance Florentine artists, such as Mariotto di Cristofano's splendid panel showing *Episodes from the Life of Christ and the Virgin*; Domenico di Michelino's *Three Archangels and Tobias* and his *Holy Trinity*; the most interesting work, however, is the *Adimari Dower Chest*, which depicts — in delightful detail — a wedding ceremony in 15th century Florence. II — Beautiful paintings including a *Visitation*, by Perugino; a *Thebaid*, attributed to Paolo Uccello and a *Madonna and Child with Angels*, by Sandro Botticelli. III — Among the works in this room, ones eyes are drawn to the exquisite *Madonna of the Sea*, attributed to Sandro Botticelli: see also a *Resurrection*, by Raffaellino del Garbo, and *Adoration*, by Lorenzo di Credi and a *Lamentation over the dead Christ*, by Jacopo del Sellaio.

THE BARTOLINI ROOM OR SALONE DELLE TOSCANE — It is to the left of the David "Tribuna", behind a glass door. It contains a collection of workshop plastercasts by Lorenzo Bartolini, one of the most important sculptors of the Romantic and post-Neoclassical periods, who was appointed official Court Sculptor by Napoleon (see: *busts of Byron, Liszt, funeral monument of the Countess Sophia Czartorysky* etc.).

BYZANTINE ROOMS — I — To the left of the David "Tribuna"; the first room contains 13th century Tuscan School panel paintings, such as two fragments from

The Academy Gallery — The Bartolini Plaster-cast Hall.

an altarpiece and the great panel painting of the *Magdalen*, by the Master of the Magdalen; a great Sienese wooden *Crucifix*; and the magnificent *Tree of the Cross* by Pacino di Buonaguida, as well as a polyptych with a *Crucifixion and Saints*. II — Contains 14th century Florentine School painting. It includes a lovely polyptych by Bernardo Daddi, showing the *Coronation of the Virgin*; a great wooden 13th century Florentine *Crucifix*, as well as a polyptych showing the *Madonna and Child with Saints*, by Orcagna. III — Here we find a School of Bernardo Daddi wooden *Crucifix* and the tragic *Lamentation over the dead Christ*, by Giovanni da Milano: a *Madonna and Child*, by Taddeo Gaddi; a number of paintings by the Master of the Rinuccini Chapel and *Stories from the Life of Christ and St. Francis*, from the Sacristy of Santa Croce.

FIRST FLOOR ROOMS — These rooms were opened to the public in June 1985. They contain a large collection of Florentine 14th and 15th century paintings which had been entrusted to the Academy Gallery and have now been beautifully arranged and lit in these upper rooms. I — The first room contains two remarkable painted *Crosses*, by Lorenzo Monaco: a splendid polyptych, by Mariotto di Nardo, from the Convent of San Gaggio: other works by Giovanni Bonsi, Nicolò di Pietro Gerini, Bernardo Daddi, etc. II — A few steps lead up to this long gallery, which contains the largest number of polyptychs ever assembled in one room. The sight is extremely impressive, thanks moreover to the perfect illumination. To mention but a few: a *Presentation at the Temple* and an *Annunciation*, by Giovanni del Biondo; a *Pentecost*, by Spinello Aretino; the *Coronation of the Virgin*, by Rossello di Jacopo Franchi and many others. III — The third hall is full of works of the most varied provenance: a remarkably rich collection of *Russian icons*, most of which were cleaned in expectation of the opening of these rooms. One of the most interesting items is a *Saint-Day Calendar* divided into two panels according

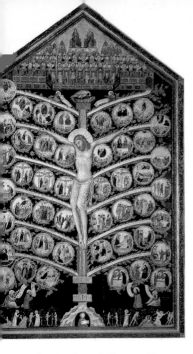

The Academy Gallery — The tree of life, by Pacino di Bonaguida and a Lamentation of Christ, surrounded by symbols of the Passion, by Lorenzo Monaco; *below*: Madonna and Child with Saints, by Spinello Aretino.

Piazza Santissima Annunziata with the church of the Santissima Annunziata on the left.

to the months September – February and March – August. IV – This room is dedicated to the International Gothic style, which is represented by Agnolo Gaddi, Lorenzo Monaco, Mariotto di Nardo, etc.

PIAZZA SANTISSIMA ANNUNZIATA

This square, of perfect proportions and dimensions, is a perfect setting for which enhance rather than dwarf man, embodies the true essence of the Renaissance spirit. Bounded on three sides by lovely arcades, the square an *equestrian statue of Grandduke Ferdinando I*, a late work designed by Giambologna and cast by Pietro Tacca (1608), and for two elegant Baroque *fountains with bronze sea monsters*, by Tacca and helpers (1629). To the right of the church of Santissima Annunziata is Brunelleschi's *Spedale degli Innocenti* (Foundling Hospital), while on the left is the **Confraternita dei Servi di Maria**, by Antonio da Sangallo the Elder and Baccio d'Agnolo (1516-1525), where the arcade echoes the elegant lines of Brunelleschi's across the square.

HOSPITAL OF THE INNOCENTS

In 1419 the Silk Merchants Guild decided to acquire a tract of land for a Hospital for the foundlings or "innocents" of the city. The project was

Hospital of the Innocents — The two Brunelleschi cloisters inside the building.

entrusted to Filippo Brunelleschi in 1411, and the building was concluded in 1457 by Francesco della Luna. The façade of the building consists of nine wide arches supported by columns standing on a podium led up to by a series of steps. The first floor is low-ceilinged with harmonious architraved windows. Between each arch there is a series of ten roundels of enamelled terracotta, by Andrea della Robbia showing *new-born babies* in swaddling clothes (c. 1487). Below the loggia, there are some frescoes by Poccetti and in the lunette above the left door, the *Holy Father with the Martyred Innocents*, by Giovanni di Francesco (1458).

There are two extraordinarily elegant Brunelleschi cloisters within the building, and a **Gallery** of paintings and sculpture which are mostly 15th century. Among the paintings worth mentioning in the collection are: an *Annunciation*, by Giovanni del Biondo; a *Madonna and Child with Saints*, by Piero di Cosimo; an *Adoration of the Magi*, by Ghirlandaio (1488); a Perugino workshop *Madonna and Child with Angels*; a *Madonna of the Innocents*, attributed to Pontormo and a *St. Sebastian*, by Andrea del Sarto.

SANTISSIMA ANNUNZIATA

Inside this church is the much venerated holy image of the Virgin known as the *"Madonna Annunziata"* (the Virgin Annunciate). Originally built around 1250 by the seven monks who founded the order of the Servants of Mary, the church was restructured by Michelozzo in 1444 and then again in the 17th and 18th centuries. The seven-arched porch leading to

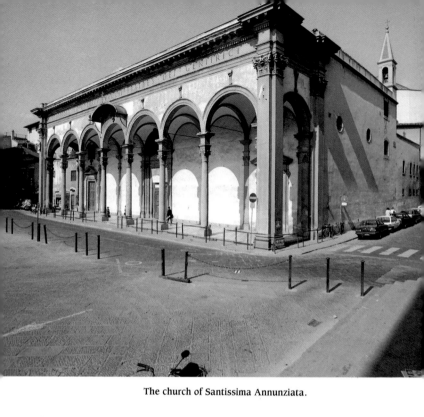

The church of Santissima Annunziata.

the church proper was built in 1601 by Giovanni Caccini. The central arch, with a fresco by Pontormo portraying Charity and Faith, is earlier than the others and has been attributed to Antonio da Sangallo the Elder.

The arcade leads to an atrium known as the **Chiostrino dei Voti** built by Antonio Martinetti in 1447 after Michelozzo's design. The subjects of the interesting frescoes in the arches are (starting from the one to the right of the entrance): the *Assumption* by Giovanni Battista Rosso (1517) the *Visitation* by Pontormo (1516) the *Marriage of the Virgin* by Franciabigio (1513), a relief carving of the *Virgin* by Michelozzo, the *Birth of the Virgin*, one of Andrea del Sarto's best-known works (1514), the *Three Magi*, also by del Sarto (1513), The *Nativity* by Alessio Baldovinetti (1462, and thus the oldest fresco here), the *Vocation of St. Filippo Benizzi* by Cosimo Rosselli (1476), and others with *episodes from the life of St. Filippo Benizzi* by Andrea del Sarto. There is a *bust of Andrea del Sarto* by Caccini on the wall.

THE INTERIOR — The interior reflects the Baroque taste for elaborate decoration. Aisleless, it has deep side chapels and a carved ceiling adorned with stuccowork. To the left of the entrance is a marble **Temple** designed by Michelozzo (1448) and built by Lapo Portigiani. It protects an elaborate altar which contains a miraculous image of the Virgin (generally veiled). According to legend, the image — a 14th century Florentine school panel of no particular merit — was actually painted by a certain Bartolomeo who fell asleep over his work only to find that an angel had painted in the Virgin's head in the meantime. The hanging lamps, candlesticks, silver altar and altarfront were donated by the Medici granddukes. — In the first

Santissima Annunziata — The Chiostrino dei Voti (the little cloister of the Vows).

chapel on the left, *St. Julian*, remains of a fresco by Andrea del Castagno. In the second chapel, the *Trinity, the three Marys, and St. Jerome* by Andrea del Castagno. In the fourth chapel, the *Assumption of the Virgin* by Perugino and helpers. In the *Chapel of the Crucifix* in the left transept is a terracotta statue of *St. John the Baptist* by Michelozzo. The corridor on the right leads to the **Sacristy** designed by Michelozzo and built by Lapo Portigiani. In the **Rotunda**: the fresco in the dome of the *Coronation of the Virgin* is by Volterrano. On the left is the *tomb of Bishop Angelo Marzi Medici* by Francesco da Sangallo (1546). On the floor is the *tomb slab of Andrea del Sarto*. Behind the choir, the centre chapel, the **Chapel of Mercy** (Soccorso), was designed by Giambologna as a burial place for himself and the other Flemish artists who died in Florence. The *crucifix* on the altar and the bronze bas-reliefs depicting *scenes of the Passion* are also by Giambologna. The chapel on the left contains a *Resurrection* by Bronzino and a wooden *statue of St. Roch* by the Nuremberg sculptor, Viet Stoss. To the right of the rotunda is the *tomb of Donato dell'Antella* by G. B. Foggini. In the fifth chapel on the right, a *monument to Orlando dei Medici* by Bernardo Rossellino (1456). In the fourth chapel, a marble *Pietà* by Baccio Bandinelli who is buried here (1559). From the left transept, by way of the door opposite the sacristy, we enter the **Chiostro dei Morti** (Cloister of the Dead). Above the north door is a famous fresco by Andrea del Sarto, the *Madonna of the Sack*. The cloister walls are covered with frescoes showing episodes from the history of the Order of the Servants of Mary, many of which were painted by Bernardino Poccetti. Beneath the portico is the entrance to the **Chapel of St. Luke**, since 1562 headquarters of the *"Compagnia degli Artisti Fiorentini"* (the artists' guild). Among the artists buried here are Benvenuto Cellini, Franciabigio, and Pontormo.

Archaeological Museum — Mater Matuta.

THE ARCHAEOLOGICAL MUSEUM

The museum housed in the Crocetta Palace, shelters one of the finest collections of archeological pieces to be found in Italy. The three major divisions are the Etruscan, the Egyptian and the Etrusco-Greek-Roman sections.

On the ground floor are two recently arranged rooms. The first features the renowned *François vase* displayed in the center of the room. This masterpiece of 6th century B.C. Attic figure painting decorated with mythological scenes, is signed by the potter Ergotimos and the painter Kleitias. The photos and explanatory notes on the walls document the painstaking steps in the restoration of the vase. In the second room are four Etruscan funerary urns from Chiusi and Chianciano, one of which, is the famous *Mater Matuta*. Photos and explanatory texts provide valuable information on the exhibits.

The Egyptian Museum — The collection, second only to the Turin collection, was founded in 1824. It is composed of the finds excavated under the supervision

Archaeological Museum – The Chimaera of Arezzo.

of Ippolito Rossellini, as well as pieces donated by private collectors. The eight-room museum has a vast collection of sarcophagi, mummies, sculpture, jewelry, papyri, etc. of different periods. The highlights are: a fragment from a granite sculpture with the Goddess Hathor as a cow nuturing the Pharoah Harembeb (14th century B.C.), a bust of a pharoah in red basalt (13th century B.C.), a painted relief of the Goddess Hathor holding out her hand to the Pharoah Sethos (13th century B.C.), two statuettes of young girls making beer and a third grinding flour (1625-2475 B.C.), and a wood and bone chariot found in a necropolis at Thebes (14th century B.C.).

The Etrusco-Greek-Roman Antiquarium – The collection is made up of pieces originally part of the Medici and Lorraine granddukes' private collections, further enriched by bequests and purchases. It consists mainly of sculptures and bronzes. The most important exhibits are: the *sarcophagus of Ramta Uznai* (1st century B.C.), the *Minerva from Arezzo* (school of Praxiteles), the *Chimera from Arezzo* (the Etruscan, 5th century B.C.), the *Haranguer* (statue honouring a prominent Etruscan, Aulus Metellus, dated around the 3rd-2nd century B.C.), the *Idolino* (Greek original of the 5th century B.C.), *Horse's head* (this Hellenistic work inspired the horse of Donatello's famous Gattamelata equestrian monument which the great artist erected in Padua). – On the same floor are the Coin and Jewel

Archaeological Museum — One of the rooms of the Egyptian Collection with mummies and sarcophagi.

Collection (gemstones, cameos, silver, etc.). On the third floor are the Etrusco-Greek-Roman collections. The works exhibited come from both northern and southern Italy, Cyprus, Crete, Greece, and Rhodes, including an extensive collection of 6th century B.C. Attic and black figure vases. Etruscan ceramics, frescoes detached from Etruscan tombs, reproductions of Etruscan painting from Vulci, Tarquinia, and Chiusi tombs, and the painted sarcophagus of Larthis Seiantus (3rd-2nd century B.C.).

Via della Colonna flanks the whole length of the Archeological Museum. On the right side of the street, where it intersects Via della Pergola, is Cellini's house.

Monastery of Santa Maria Maddalena de' Pazzi — (Via della Colonna 7; if it is closed, ring for the custodian). In the Chapter Room of this old monastery is Perugino's famous fresco depicting the *Crucifixion*. The harmonious composition, divided by the arches into three parts, is enhanced by the superb background landscape. In the center is the Crucifixion scene with St. Mary Magdalen in adoration flanked by the Virgin and St. Bernard on the left and Sts. John and Benedict on the right.

The road ends in Piazza d'Azeglio, a large square built around an extensive garden full of tall plane trees. On ones right one turns into via Farini.

The Sinagogue — at Nr. 6, Via Farini. It was built in 1872-74 and designed by the architects Mariano Falcini, Gaddo Treves and Vincenzo Micheli, thanks chiefly

Synagogue — Overall view of the exterior.

to a considerable legacy bequeathed by David Levi, who had been an important member of the Jewish community of Florence in the 19th century. The style reflects the Sephardic type of Moorish – influenced decoration. The domes are covered in copper and the interior is profusely decorated with geometrical patterns of great effect.

Via Farini leads into via dei Pilastri, from where one can turn into piazza Sant'Ambrogio.

The Church of Sant'Ambrogio – Although the original structure dates from 1296, is has since been restructured. Inside the aisless church are several superb Renaissance altars and 14th-15th century paintings. The *Chapel of the Miracle* to the left of the choir has a fine tabernacle by Mino da Fiesole (1481), a fresco with a *Procession* by Cosimo Rosselli (1486), and, on the next wall, a painting of *Angels and saints* by Alessio Baldovinetti. On the floor, a plaque indicates where Mino da Fiesole is buried. Among the other famous artists buried here are Andrea del Verrocchio, Simone del Pollaiuolo (Cronaca), and Francesco Granacci.

SIXTH ITINERARY

Piazza del Duomo — Via del Proconsolo — Dante's House — Piazza San Firenze — Bargello Palace (National Museum) — Badia Church — Michelangelo's House — Piazza and Church of Santa Croce (Pazzi Chapel; Santa Croce Museum) — Horne Museum — Bardini Museum.

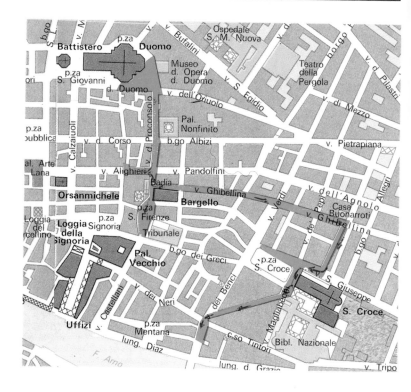

Via del Proconsolo — This street, which starts on the south side of the Cathedral apse, is one of the oldest in the city (it dates from Roman times). A few yards down is a tiny square, Piazza Santa Maria del Campo, with the church of the same name. Number 12, at the intersection of Borgo degli Albizi, is the so-called **Palazzo Nonfinito** (Unfinished Palace). Begun by Bernardo Buontalenti in 1593 (it was commissioned by Alessandro Strozzi), the project was taken up by G. B. Caccini, then continued by Matteo Nigetti, and others, yet was never completed by anybody. Today it is the **Museum of Anthropology and Ethnology** founded by Paolo Mantegazza and featuring collections relating to African, Asian, Indonesian, Oceanic, and American civilizations. Along the street, at number 10, is a superb example of the Renaissance palace, **Palazzo Pazzi-Quaratesi**, designed by Giuliano da Maiano for the Pazzi family. Further on, we turn right into Via Dante Alighieri which has a picturesque cluster of old buildings midway

160

The Bargello Palace (the National Museum of Sculpture).

along it. On the corner is a much-restored building known as the **House of Dante**, supposedly where Dante was born. Continuing along Via del Proconsolo we see the church of the Badia on the right and across the street, the Palazzo del Bargello, now the National Museum. A few yards further down is Piazza San Firenze.

Piazza San Firenze — With our backs to the 16th century side of Palazzo Vechio, we get a splendid view of the Bargello with its plain fortress-like façade and sturdy 12th century tower. Opposite it, the slender belltower of the Badia rises out of a cluster of lower buildings, while in the background we see the unmistakable shape of Brunelleschi's dome. On the west side of the square is **Palazzo Gondi**, one of the finest examples of Italian Renaissance architecture. Designed by Giuliano da Sangallo in 1494, the building also contains a remarkable courtyard. Opposite is a Baroque complex, comprising a central core flanked by a church on either side. Formerly the monastery of the order St. Filippo Neri, the building is today used as the Law-courts of Florence, whereas the church on the left is still consecrated to St. Firenze.

The Bargello Palace — The courtyard and outer staircase.

BARGELLO PALACE
(or NATIONAL MUSEUM OF SCULPTURE)

Together with Palazzo Vecchio, which was built 43 years later, the most important non-religious building in medieval Florence. The front part — overlooking via del Proconsolo — is the oldest and was founded in 1255; the rear section, abutting on via della Vigna Vecchia and Via dell'Acqua was, on the other hand, built between 1325 and 1346. The great battlemented tower, known as the Volognana, was built before the palace, in the 12th century. The bell, called the "Montanina", which was removed from the castle of Montale, when the latter was taken by the Florentines in 1302, and has since hung in the Volognana tower, was the alarm bell rung to call the Florentines to arms or assembly, in cases of public emergency or danger. The palace used to be the seat of the Captain

The Bargello Palace – Partial views of the portico and veranda.

of the People, then of the Podestà (governor). As from 1574 it became the headquarters of the Captain of Justice or Bargello (or head of the police). The building thereafter was used as a prison, where the condemned were incarcerated, tortured and executed on the gallows, erected in the centre of the courtyard. After the post of Bargello was decreed obsolete, during the last century, the palace was restored and restructured and it was decided to use it as headquarters of the **National Museum**. The Bargello now contains the most important collection of Renaissance sculpture in Florence, as well as interesting maiolica, coins, arms and armour, medieval ivory, enamels, paintings, jewellery, etc.

GROUND FLOOR - COURTYARD – Access to the courtyard is through the vestibule where tickets are sold. Beneath the arcade are several 16th century Florentine statues. Of particular interest: a number of *allegorical figures* sculpted by Bartolomeo Ammannati and a reconstruction of a *fountain* from the Boboli Gardens, by the same. Other fine works include a statue of *Fiesole* by Tribolo (16th cent.) and the *Fisherboy* by the 19th century sculptor Vincenzo Gemito. The imposing staircase designed by Neri di Fioravante, beautifully completes the architectural setting. All over the walls and beneath the arcades are the coat-of-arms of *Podestà* (governors) and magistrates as well as the painted emblems of the various sections of the city.

THE 14TH CENTURY HALL – Access is from the courtyard, opposite the entrance. The room contains 14th century Tuscan sculpture. Immediately to the right, the *statue of Alfonso of Aragon*, in an extraordinarily human and pathetically slumped posture, attributed to Francesco Laurana.

163

THE 16TH CENTURY HALL — Immediately to the right of the entrance, next to the foot of the external staircase in the courtyard, one enters the great hall divided by massive piers which contains Tuscan sculpture of the 16th century. Among the various works by Michelangelo Buonarroti, the *Apollo-David*; the powerful *Bust of Brutus*; the *Bacchus*, one of his earliest works and the lovely *Madonna and Child*, known as the Pitti Tondo, which is the sculptured counterpart to the painted Doni Tondo in the Uffizi Gallery. The hall also contains the marvellous Bust of Cosimo Ist de' Medici, and the statuettes of *Danae and her son Perseus, Perseus, Minerva, Mercury, Jupiter* and the panel of *Perseus freeing Andromeda*, all cast in bronze by Benvenuto Cellini; see also: Jacopo Sansovino's *Bacchus*, together with Giambologna's world-famous *Mercury* as well as his *Florence victorious over Pisa*, plus works by Bandinelli, Ammannati and the *Bust of Michelangelo*, by Daniele da Volterra.

THE FIRST FLOOR — On a pillar by the staircase is the *seated lion* known as the *Marzocco*, the symbol of Republican Florence. Upstairs on the loggia (*verone*) is a collection of Giambologna's extraordinary sculptures, including his realistic *animal figures* and his *Architecture*.

THE MAIN HALL — This striking room used to be the *Salone del Consiglio Grande* (the Great Council Hall). It contains some of the most famous Early Renaissance sculptures of 15th century Florence, especially the revolutionary creations of Donatello, the foremost *Quattrocento* sculptor. Just as Masaccio brought new ideas to painting, Donatello initiated the new course of sculpture. His freestanding figures, including the bronze David, the first nude since antiquity, are anatomically accurate and naturalistically posed, unlike the stiffer, hieratic Gothic and Romanesque statues that preceded them. His *"stiacciato"* reliefs (a relief consisting of shallowly incised lines) convey the effect of paintings and his use of perspective in them even precedes Masacco. His *St. George* (1416) dominates the whole hall from its niche on the end-wall, next to it: a *Crucifixion* in bas-relief. Along the end-wall there are three beautiful painted 15th century Florentine *dower chests*. We can also admire an early marble *David* and the famous bronze *David* of 1430, as well as two versions of *St. John the Baptist*, one of which is an early work, while the other is a late one. The works by the other sculptors here, especially those by Desiderio da Settignano (e.g. *bust of St. John*) all reveal Donatello's enormous influence on 15th century sculpture. In addition, you can see and compare the famous reliefs showing the *Sacrifice of Isaac* that Ghiberti and Brunelleschi prepared in 1402 for the competition of the Baptistry door (won by Ghiberti). Other highlights include a painted plaster relief of the *Virgin and Child with angels* by Agostino di Duccio, two glazed terracottas of the *Virgin* by Luca della Robbia and a bronze relief of a *Battle scene* by Bertoldo.

THE SALA DELLA TORRE (Tower Room) — In addition to embroidered fabrics and tapestries, there are ivories, silver, as well as arms and armour of varied provenance from the Grandducal collections.

THE SALA DEL PODESTÀ (Governor's Room) — These enamels, crystalware, and 16th century Venetian, French, and Oriental art treasures originally belonged to the French art collector, M. Louis Carrand, who donated them to the city of Florence in 1888. Of particular note are the Limoges enamels from the 11th to 14th centuries displayed in the first and last showcases.

THE PODESTÀ'S CHAPEL — People sentenced to death spent their last few hours in prayer in this chapel. The frescoes on the walls, sometimes attributed to Giotto show *Hell* (by the entrance), *scenes from the life of St. Mary Magdalen, St. Mary of Egypt, and St. John the Baptist* (along the sides) *and Paradise* (far wall),

The Bargello Palace — Donatello's David; Verrocchio's David (*right*); *below*: Lorenzo Ghiberti's Abraham sacrificing Isaac and Filippo Brunelleschi's Abraham sacrificing Isaac (*right*).

where a (much-repainted) portrait of Dante is visible. The painting of the *Virgin and Child with four Saints* is by Giovanni di Franco. In the showcases are chalices, ecclesiastical ornaments and reliquaries of 13th and 14th century Tuscan craftmanship.

SACRISTY OF THE CHAPEL — This room was rearranged in 1987. It contains portable altars, reliquiaries and an *Enamelled Crucifix* by Antonio del Pollaiuolo.

THE IVORY ROOM (Collection of Ivories) — This is one of the world's finest collection of medieval ivories. In the room are also fine pieces of 14th and 15th century Tuscan wood sculpture.

The Bargello Palace — The bust of Brutus, by Michelangelo and Lady with a nosegay, by Verrocchio.

THE GLASS AND MAJOLICA ROOM — This collection features pieces from the famous pottery works of Faenza, Pesaro, Urbino, and Florence, as well as interesting 16th century Moorish style ceramics from the factory of Valencia.

SECOND FLOOR — THE GIOVANNI DELLA ROBBIA ROOM — Among the fine pieces displayed here, two by Giovanni della Robbia, the *Pietà* and the *Noli me tangere*, are particularly outstanding. In addition, there is a bust of *Costanza Bonarelli* by Bernini, the Roman Baroque master, and the *Ganymede*, an antique statue restored by Benvenuto Cellini.

THE ARMOURY (Arms and Armour Collection) — The weapons dating from various periods displayed here mostly belonged to the Medici collections.

THE DELLA ROBBIA ROOM — These glazed terracottas are by Andrea, Luca, and Giovanni della Robbia and Santi Buglioni.

THE VERROCCHIO ROOM — This room features sculpture by the Florentine artist Andrea de' Cione called Verrocchio (b. 1435-d. 1488) to whom Leonardo da Vinci was apprenticed. The sculptures include the charming bronze *David*, a *bust of a lady with a nosegay*, two versions of the *Virgin*, one in terracotta and one in marble, a *bust of Piero di Lorenzo dei Medici*, and a relief of the *Death of Francesca Pitti Tornabuoni*. There are also fine sculptures by Antonio Rossellino, Mino da Fiesole, Benedetto da Maiano, Antonio del Pollaiuolo, Francesco Laurana, and Matteo Cividali.

THE FIREPLACE ROOM — The room is named after the 16th century carved fireplace from Palazzo Borgherini by Benedetto da Rovezzano. Other Renaissance sculptors represented are Ghiberti, Antonio del Pollaiuolo, Tacca, and M. Soldani. Giambologna's *Labours of Hercules* and the model for his famous *Mercury* are also displayed.

The Bargello Palace — Two della Robbia Madonnas.

BADIA FIORENTINA

This Benedectine church was founded in the 10th century by Countess Willa, mother of Ugo, the Margrave of Tuscany. It was enlarged in 1285 — the outer wing dates from this time — and then completely restructured in the Baroque style by Matteo Segaloni in the 1620s. Above the elaborate *portal* (by Benedetto da Rovezzano, 1495), is a glazed terracotta lunette of the *Virgin and Child* by Benedetto Buglioni (15th century). Benedetto da Rovezzano also designed the Corinthian portico and vestibule to the church. From the portico you get a fine view of the 14th century belltower.

The interior, in the shape of a Greek cross, is dominated by a wonderful carved cedar-wood *ceiling*. Designed by Matteo Segaloni in 1625, the ceiling was carved by Felice Gamberai and Domenico Dotti. Major Renaissance works are to be found here. To the right is the *wall tomb of Giannozzo Pandolfini* (workshop of Bernardo Rossellini); next to it, a bas-relief sculpted by Mino da Fiesole (1464-1469) as an altar-front with the *Virgin and Child blessing with Sts. Laurence and Leonard*. In the right transept is the *tomb of Bernardo Giugni* by Mino (c. 1468) and, in the left one, Mino's masterpiece, the beautifully carved *tomb of Ugo, Margrave of Tuscany* (1469-1481). Above the tomb is a painting of the *Assumption* by Vasari. The next chapel is frescoed with *scenes of the Passion* traditionally attributed to Buffalmacco, but actually by an unknown follower of Giotto. Just to the left of the church entrance is one of Filippino Lippi's finest works, the *Virgin appearing to St. Bernard* (1480). To the right of the choir is a door leading to the 15th century **Chiostro degli Aranci** (Cloister of the Orange Trees), a lovely two storey loggia. In the upper level are interesting frescoes of the story of St. Benedict attributed to the Portuguese painter, Consalvo.

Opposite the church is Via Ghibellina, with the Bargello on the righthand corner, Buonarroti's house is at Via Ghibellina, 70.

Michelangelo's House — The Madonna of the Stairs and the wooden Crucifix, both early works by Michelangelo.

The Casa Buonarroti (Michelangelo's House) — Purchased by Michelangelo, the house was transformed into a museum by his heirs. In the first floor rooms are youthful works by the master, including a famous relief of the *Battle of the Lapiths and the Centaurs* and a *Virgin and Child* known as the *"Madonna di San Lorenzo."* There is also an original *bronze portrait bust of Michelangelo* by Daniele da Volterra. The adjoining room has a display of drawings, studies of nudes, portraits, and architectural designs. Also on the first floor is the delicate wooden *Crucifix*, carved for the abbot of Santo Spirito by young Michelangelo. Elsewhere in the museum are two other *portraits of the artist*, one by Bugiardini and one by Venusti, and a *portrait of Vittoria Colonna*, Michelangelo's closest friend, attributed to Pontormo.

Opposite Casa Buonarroti is Via delle Pinzochere which leads directly into Piazza Santa Croce.

PIAZZA SANTA CROCE

This square, more than any other in the city, has been witness to the changing lifestyles of the Florentine people. Here, early in the city's

The church of Santa Croce overlooking its spacious square.

history, the people assembled to listen to preachers recounting the Gospel, here in the 15th century they came to watch the jousting matches of the noble knights (an unforgettable joust won by Giuliano de' Medici was even immortalized in verse by Poliziano), here throughout the 16th century they cheered their favorite football teams, playing in the rough, violent game of the Calcio in Costume (Football in Costume). One side of the square is bounded by the church, the others by old buildings, the two most interesting of which are No. 1, **Palazzo Cocchi-Serristori**, designed by Baccio d'Agnolo in 1470 and No. 21, **Palazzo dell'Antella**, built by Giulio Parigi in 1617. The striking façade of the latter is covered with frescoes painted in only 27 days by a team of 12 painters under the supervision of Giovanni da San Giovanni.

SANTA CROCE

This church, which is one of the foremost Franciscan churches in Italy, rises on the site of a much more modest church, also Franciscan, which once stood here. The construction of the huge basilica started in the second half of the 13th century and continued up to the end of the 14th century. The result is a masterpiece of Tuscan Gothic architecture, often

Santa Croce — Interior.

attributed to the genius of Arnolfo di Cambio, the architect who designed Palazzo Vecchio and the Cathedral. The marble façade is a 19th century addition (1857-1863) by Niccolò Matas. The Virgin above the central portal and the *Triumph of the Cross* in the lunette below are by Giovanni Duprè. The *Finding of the True Cross* in the lefthand portal lunette, by Tito Sarrocchi, while the *Vision of Constantine* on the opposite side is by Zocchi. The graceful belfry designed by Gaetano Baccani in 1865 was inspired by the Gothic style. To the left of the steps leading up to the church is a *Statue of Dante Alighieri* by Enrico Pazzi (19th cent.).

THE INTERIOR — The ground plan is an Egyptian or Tau-cross. There are two side-aisles separated from the nave by a series of ogival arches supported on octagonal stone piers. There are *276 tombstones* embedded in the terracotta floor (the most ancient dating from the 14th century).

INNER FAÇADE — The splendid stained-glass rose window shows a *Deposition*, probably based on a cartoon by Giovanni da Ponte; right: *monument to Gino Capponi*, by Bortone (1884); left: *monument to Giovan Battista Niccolini*, by Pio Fedi (1883).

NAVE — On the third right pier, a splendid marble **pulpit** by Benedetto da Maiano, with five panels sculpted in relief depicting *Episodes from the Life of St. Francis* (1476).

RIGHT AISLE — Antonio Rossellino's charming *Madonna del Latte* (Virgin of the Milk) of 1478 is on the first pillar. Opposite is *Michelangelo's Tomb* by Vasari (1564). Beyond the 2nd altar is the *Cenotaph of Dante* (who however is buried in

Santa Croce — View down the right aisle; *below*: the Pulpit, by Benedetto da Maiano and Michelangelo's Tomb, by Giorgio Vasari.

Santa Croce – Sacristy.

Ravenna) by Ricci (1839), beyond the 3rd altar, Canova's neo-Classical *monument to Vittorio Alfieri* (the playwright) and beyond the 4th altar is a *monument to Niccolò Machiavelli*, by Innocenzo Spinazzi (1787). To the left of the 5th altar and the *tomb of Luigi Lanzi* (the historian) by Giuseppe Belli (1810) is an exquisite Renaissance tabernacle framing a relief of the *Annunciation*, of *pietra serena*. It ranks as one of Donatello's finest works (1435). Just beyond the door leading into the cloister is another landmark of Renaissance sculpture, indeed the prototype of all Renaissance wall monuments, the *tomb of Leonardo Bruni* (the famed humanist and chancellor of the Republic). It is the masterpiece of Bernardo Rossellino (mid-15th century). Next is the *tomb of Rossini* (the composer) by Giuseppe Cassioli (1886). Rossini died in Paris in 1868 and eighteen years later his body was brought here. Beyond the last altar is the *tomb of Ugo Foscolo* (the poet) with a statue by Antonio Berti (1939).

RIGHT TRANSEPT — On the extreme right is the **Cappella Castellani** (or *Cappella del Sacramento*) decorated with a 14th century fresco cycle by Agnolo Gaddi and Gerardo Starnina, among others. On the right are the *stories of St. Nicholas of Bari* and *St. John the Baptist*, while the *lives of St. John the Evangelist* and *St. Anthony Abbot* are recounted on the left. The painted wooden *crucifix* is by Niccolò Gerini (1386). The pillar statues of *St. Francis* and *St. Dominic* are della Robbia terracottas. At the end of the transept is the **Cappella Baroncelli** decorated with Taddeo Gaddi's marvellous fresco cycle illustrating the *life of Mary* (1338). Although the *Coronation of the Virgin* on the altar bears the signature of Giotto, it is probably a workshop piece. The fresco of the *Virgin handing her girdle to St. Thomas* is by Sebastiano Mainardi (c. 1490). Outside the chapel, on the righthand side, is the *tomb of a member of the Baroncelli family* attributed to Giovanni di Balduccio of Siena (14th century). Next is a doorway which leads into a barrel-vaulted corridor, both of which were designed by Michelozzo. The door on the left leads to the 14th century **Sacristy** decorated

Santa Croce — The Main Chapel

with frescoes of *stories of the Passion* attributed to Niccolò di Piero Gerini (late 14th century). The exquisite inlaid cabinets by Giovanni di Michele (1454) and Nanni Ungaro (1530) contain priceless illuminated missal books, ecclesiastical fittings, and relics of St. Francis. A Gothic wrought-iron grille encloses the **Rinuccini Chapel**, frescoed with the *stories of the Virgin and Mary Magdalen* by

Giovanni da Milano and helpers (1366). The altarpiece of the *Virgin surrounded by Saints* is by Giovanni del Biondo (1379). Reentering the corridor, we turn left until we reach the **Cappella dei Medici**, also designed by Michelozzo (1434). It contains a fine tabernacle by Mino da Fiesole (1474), a bas-relief attributed to Donatello, and, on the altar, a superb glazed terracotta, by Andrea della Robbia of the *Virgin and Child with saints* (c. 1480).

THE CHAPELS OF THE EAST END — The eleven chapels along the east end of the church were commissioned by the foremost Florentine families. Each one is named after its sponsor and consecrated to the family's patron saint. Starting from the right, the 1st chapel is the **Cappella Velluti** (which later passed into the hands of the Morelli and Riccardi families), bearing traces of frescoes of the *story of St. Michael the Archangel* by a pupil of Cimabue. The 2nd chapel, the **Cappella dei Bellacci**, frescoed by Taddeo Gaddi, was repainted by Gherardo Silvani in the 17th century. The 3rd, the **Cappella dei Silvestri**, later **Cappella Bonaparte**, contains a *monument to Charlotte Bonaparte* by Lorenzo Bartolini. The 4th is the **Cappella Peruzzi** with a major fresco cycle painted by Giotto, after 1320 that was whitewashed over, and then brought back to light and poorly restored — and repainted — in the mid 1800s (it has been recently cleaned and restored again). On the righthand wall are *scenes from the life of St. John the Evangelist*. Starting from the upper register they are the *Vision on the isle of Patmos*, the *Raising of Drusiana*, and *St. John ascends to Heaven*. On the left wall are *scenes from the life of St. John the Baptist*. From above: *Zacharias and the Angel*, the *birth of St. John*, and *Herod's feast with Salome presenting the head of the Baptist*. By the windows are figures of *saints*, while the four *Evangelists* are represented on the ceiling. The 5th chapel is the famous **Cappella Bardi** in which Giotto painted a fresco cycle on the *life of St. Francis*. The frescoes were rediscovered in 1853 and restored a bit more skillfully than those in the Peruzzi Chapel. Outside the chapel are *St. Francis receiving the Stigmata* and two medallions of *Adam* and *Eve*. On the left wall starting from the top: *St. Francis giving up his worldly possessions, the saint appearing to St. Anthony preaching in Arles*, and the *death of St. Francis*. Opposite, from the top: *St. Francis giving the Rule to the order, being tried by fire before the Sultan*, and *Visions of the monk Agostino and Bishop Guido*. In the vaults are allegorical figures of *Poverty, Obedience, Chastity*, and *St. Francis in Glory*. On the far wall are *Sts. Louis of Toulouse, Elizabeth, and Clair*. The *altarpiece*, a delightful rendition of the life of St. Francis is attributed to a painter from Lucca, Bonaventura Berlinghieri, a contemporary of the saint (end of the 13th century). The **Main Chapel** (or **Cappella Alberti**) was frescoed by Angolo Gaddi with the *Legend of the True Cross* (1380). The altarpiece with the *Virgin and Child is by Niccolò Gerini. The four Fathers of the Church* are by Nardo di Cione. The great *crucifix* is by a master of the Giotto circle. The 7th chapel, the **Chappella Tosinghi** (later Spinelli and then Sloane), was once frescoed by Giotto. Of the original Life of Mary cycle only the *Assumption* on the outer arch is extant. The *altarpiece* is by Giovanni del Biondo (1372). — The *Pietà* in the 8th chapel, the **Cappella Capponi**, is a monument to the mothers of Italy. It was sculpted by Andreotti (1926). — The 9th, the **Cappella Ricasoli** has 19th century frescoes and paintings by Luigi, Giuseppe, and Francesco Sebastelli. The 10th, the **Cappella Pulci** (later Berardi and then Bardi) was frescoed by Bernardo Daddi (1330), and helpers. The subjects of the frescoes are the *Martyrdom of St. Laurence* and the *Martyrdom of St. Stephen*. The ceramic altarpiece of the *Virgin and saints* is by Giovanni della Robbia. The 11th, the **Cappella Bardi di Vernio**, was frescoed by Giotto's favorite pupil, Maso di Banco, with the *story of St. Sylvester*. The altarpiece with the *story of St. John Gualberto* was painted by Jacopo di Cione at the end of the 14th century. — The chapel at the end of the

Santa Croce — The Bardi and Peruzzi Chapels.

transept, the **Cappella Niccolini**, is a Baroque chapel designed by G. B. Dosio. In the next chapel, another **Cappella Bardi**, is the famous wooden *crucifix* by Donatello (c. 1425). On the left wall of the next chapel, the **Cappella Salviati**, is a striking wall tomb by Lorenzo Bartolini (1837).

LEFT AISLE — Between the sixth altar and the side door is the *tomb of Carlo Marsuppini*, the famous humanist. Desiderio da Settignano, who sculpted this magnificent piece around 1460, was inspired by the equally magnificent tomb carved by his teacher, Rossellino, opposite. By the fifth altar are the *tombslabs of Lorenzo and his son, Vittorio Ghiberti*. Between the first and second altars is the *tomb of Galileo Galilei* by G. B. Foggini and G. Ticciati (1737). On the walls are fragments of 14th century frescoes.

The Pazzi Chapel — Exterior.

PAZZI CHAPEL

To the right of the church of Santa Croce are the buildings of the Franciscan monastery. The first cloister is against the wall of the right aisle; the porticoes are 14th-15th century; to the right of the cloister entrance is the *monument to Florence Nightingale*, (1820-1910). At the end of the cloister one can admire the wonderful façade of the Pazzi chapel. Filippo Brunelleschi designed the building and began it (it was supposed to serve as chapterhouse of the monastery and as burial chapel for the Pazzi family) about 1430; he worked on it at intervals until 1444, then other architects completed the building. A pronaos precedes the entrance, with six Corinthian columns and a wide central arch between elegant inset panels in pietra serena; the frieze with *heads of cherubs* is by Desiderio da Settignano. The chapel has a dome with conical covering (1461) and under the portico is another small dome in coloured terracotta, by Luca della Robbia; by the same, the *Tondo of St. Andrew* above the door, the panels of which are carved by Giuliano da Maiano (1472).

The rectangular interior has the geometrical clarity and measured rhythm of the best creations of Brunelleschi: white walls, grooved pilaster strips in pietra serena, wide arches; the only touches of colour are the fine tondi by Luca della Robbia, with figures of *Apostles* and *Evangelists*. In the presbytery, a stained glass panel attributed to Alesso Baldovinetti and a small dome with *Signs of the Zodiac*. Going out into the First Cloister, a doorway on the left leads into the **Large Cloister**, designed by Brunelleschi.

SANTA CROCE MUSEUM

This small but important museum is housed in some of the rooms of the Monastery of Santa Croce. The entrance is to the right of the church.

The first, and most important of these rooms is the old 14th century Refectory; the end wall is covered by an enormous fresco by Taddeo Gaddi representing the *Tree of Life*, the *Last Supper* and other scenes; on the right wall is the great **Crucifix** painted on wood by Cimabue, badly damaged by the terrible 1966 flood, and three fragments of the *Triumph of Death* frescoed by Orcagna on the walls of Santa Croce (they were found behind Vasari's altars, and detached); on the left is the *St. Ludovic* in bronze by Donatello (1423). The remains of 14th and 15th century glass windows, by Andrea del Castagno, Agnolo Bronzino, Giorgio Vasari and others, as well as detached frescoes, reliefs, sarcophagi, etc. are kept in the other rooms.

Leaving Santa Croce, we turn left into Via Magliabechi. Along the left side of the street is the west wing of the **Biblioteca Nazionale** (State Library) which is entered from Piazza Cavalleggeri. The building, designed by Cesare Bazzini, was erected between 1911 and 1935. This world famous library, the most important in Italy, contains priceless collections of old manuscripts and historical documents. At the end of Corso Tintori, the street intersecting Via Magliabechi, we turn left into Via de' Benci. The first building on the left side, number 6, is **Palazzo degli Alberti e dei Corsi** attributed to Giuliano da Sangallo. The inner courtyard, designed by Giuliano da Sangallo presumably with the help of Andrea Sansovino, is particularly harmonious. The building is at present the head-quarters of the Horne Foundation.

HORNE MUSEUM — At the beginning of this century Herbert Percy Horne gathered together a fine collection of furniture, pictures, sculptures and other objects, in a beautiful 15th century palace in Via dei Benci that belonged to the Alberti family. Among the principal works, which the English collector donated to the Italian State, are: a stucco *Madonna* by Antonio Rossellino; a fine *Holy Family* by Beccafumi; the splendid early 15th century inlaid sacristy bench; *Madonna and Saints* by Lorenzo Monaco; the *Allegory of Music*, by Dosso Dossi; a *Madonna* and a *Pietà* both attributed to Simone Martini; the fragment of a polyptych by Pietro Lorenzetti; the magnificent *St. Stephen* by Giotto; the figure of *Esther* by Filippo Lippi; the fragment of a story of *St. Julian* by Masaccio; drawings, coins, majolica and cutlery.

Continuing down Via dei Benci towards the Arno we come to the reconstructed bridge known as **Ponte alle Grazie**. It has the same name as the bridge, destroyed during World War II, which stood near an oratory built by Jacopo degli Uberti in the 14th century to the *Madonna delle Grazie* (Our Lady of Favours) on

Museum of Santa Croce — Cimabue's great painted wooden Crucifix, damaged by the terrible 1966 flood.

the right bank of the Arno. — After crossing the bridge, we continue a few yards in the same direction to Piazza de' Mozzi. Number 1 is the Bardini Museum.

The Bardini Museum — The museum was bequeathed to the City of Florence by a Florentine antique dealer, Stefano Bardini, in 1923. The windows of the rather odd-looking mansion are actually altars taken from a church in Pistoia. The collection, over twenty rooms, covers many periods ranging from Etruscan, Greek, Roman, and 14th-15th century Italian sculpture, to paintings, tapestries, carpets, and furniture, mainly of the Renaissance period. The sculpture highlights of the collection are an *archaic Etruscan stone marker* (2nd century B.C.), a fragmentary *altar* with Bacchus and Maenads (Greek, 4th century B.C.), an allegorical *statue of Charity* attributed to Tino da Camaino, an altar base by Michelozzo, an altar frontal by Andrea della Robbia, and a terracotta *Virgin* (15th century Sienese school). The *Crucifix*, attributed to Bernardo Daddi, together with the *St. John the Baptist*, by Michele Giambono, are among the more remarkable paintings.

SEVENTH ITINERARY

Viale dei Colli – Piazzale Michelangelo – Church of San Salvator al Monte – Church of San Miniato al Monte – Viale Galileo – Via San Leonardo – Forte Belvedere.

View of the town from just below Piazzale Michelangelo, in Via dei Bastioni.

Viale dei Colli – Once you have been inside the museums and churches of Florence, you are ready for a lovely drive along the Viale dei Colli. This winding, tree-shaded avenue which skirts the southern hills that encircle the city for over four miles, affords breathtaking views of the superb Tuscan countryside with the city of Florence as a backdrop. It is rightly one of the most famous drives in Italy. Starting from Piazza Francesco Ferrucci, we take Viale Michelangelo, which gently curves between the landscaped parks of villas and mansions, until we come to Piazzale Michelanglo.

PIAZZALE MICHELANGELO

The nicest place to stop along the scenic Viale dei Colli drive is Piazzale Michelangelo. Its panoramic terrace commands an unforgettable view of Florence. Spread out along the banks of the river Arno, graced by its beautiful buildings and surrounded on all sides by the softly rolling hills.

In the background, to the left, is a big green area, the Cascine Park. Towards the right is the triple peak of Monte Morello, immediately followed by the hills of

179

View of the town from Piazzale Michelangelo.

Careggi, Montughi, and Pratolino. Practically opposite us, beyond the valley of Monte Senario, are the hills of Fiesole — the belltower of the cathedral may be easily picked out between two hills. Continuing to the right, our glance encounters Monte Ceceri and immediately, the castles dotting the Gherardo, Vincigliata and Poggio hills, coming to rest on the hill of Settignano. From our vantage point, we can see all the monuments of Florence like doll houses beneath us. On the far left (this side of the river) we can make out the belltower of Santo Spirito and the elegant dome of the church of San Frediano. Across the river is the belltower of Santa Maria Novella, while closer to us, we can see the unmistakable tower of Palazzo Vecchio. Further back is the magnificent complex of the Cathedral topped by Brunelleschi's dome and Giotto's belltower which dwarf the white-capped Baptistry beside it and the dome of the Medici Chapels of San Lorenzo slightly to the rear. In front of Giotto's belltower we can make out the tower of the Badia Church with its pointed cusp. The Bargello square, battlemented tower is slightly to the right of the Badia, and still moving our eyes right we see the belltower of Santa Croce. The green domes belong to the Synagogue. Turning to the bridges spanning the river, we shall start from the one closest to us: Ponte alle Grazie, and continue left. The next bridge, Ponte Vecchio is unmistakable; it is followed by Ponte Santa Trinita, Ponte alla Carraia, Ponte Vespucci, with Ponte alla Vittoria in the distance. To our right are Ponte San Niccolò and Ponte Giovanni da Verrazzano. Just below the terrace we are standing on is a massive tower-like structure. It is the San Niccolò Gate, built in 1324 after a design by Andrea Orcagna and was one of the strongest points in the city walls protecting the medieval city. In the middle of the square we are standing in is a monument to Michelangelo (1875) whose genius is commemorated by copies of five of his

Two views of Piazzale Michelangelo.

best-known sculptures, the David and Dusk, Dawn, Day, and Night from the Medici Tombs in San Lorenzo. The monument and the layout of the Piazzale were conceived by Giuseppe Poggi in the late 19th century. An inscription on the wall behind the little landscaped garden reads: "Giuseppe Poggi – Florentine architect – look around – this is his monument." On the hill behind Piazzale Michelangelo

The Michelangelo Monument.

is the church of San Salvatore al Monte hidden among the cypress trees. It can be reached either on foot (staircase from Viale Galileo) or by car (turn left a bit beyond the terrace beneath San Miniato al Monte).

San Salvatore al Monte — Cronaca designed this simple church, which Michelangelo called "the pretty country maid," because of the lovely simplicity of its lines — a fitting tribute to Cronaca's last work. His design is pure Renaissance: the interior is aisleless and elegantly plain, the ceiling beamed, and the apse rectangular. Several of the paintings decorating the altars date from the 15th and 16th centuries.

We reach the church of San Miniato perched on the hilltop by crossing the pleasant little park between San Salvatore and San Miniato.

SAN MINIATO AL MONTE

One of the oldest and most beautiful churches in Florence, it stands on the site of the first Christian settlements in the city, the old *Mons Florentinus*, where the woods were full, first of catacombs, then of oratories and the little hovels of the hermit-monks. One oratory was dedicated to San Miniato, who suffered martyrdom in the 4th century, and the Romanesque church was built above it in the 11th-13th centuries. The façade is covered with marble in two colours, in a clear, solemn design; the fine mosaic in the centre (13th century, much restored)

The façade of the basilica of San Miniato al Monte.

represents *Christ between the Virgin and St. Miniato*; perched on top of the tympanum, *the Eagle*, the symbol of the Guild of Woolmerchants who had undertaken to finance the upkeep of the church.

THE INTERIOR — The interior has a nave and two side aisles, with a crypt and a raised presbytery above it; the floor of the nave is set with splendid slabs of inlaid marble. In the centre, between the two flights of steps leading up to the presbytery, is the **Crucifix Chapel**, by Michelozzo (1448), commissioned by Piero the Gouty, the father of Lorenzo the Magnificent. The chapel was built to house a famous *Crucifix* which miraculously nodded to St. Giovanni Gualberto and is now in Santa Trinita; the coffered vault of the Chapel is by Luca della Robbia; on its end wall, panels painted by Agnolo Gaddi (1394). Behind the chapel, one descends into the wide **Crypt** (11th century), divided into seven aisles by slender columns surmounted by ancient capitals, some of which were remade in the 15th century. The vault of the apse is beautifully frescoed by Taddeo Gaddi. The altar is the original 11th century one and contains the bones of St. Miniato, while the lovely beaten iron grille along the top of the steps leading down into the crypt was made in the 14th century. The presbytery is surrounded by a high iconostasis with an elegant pulpit on the right; above the altar to the right of the upper apse is a painting on wooden panel by Jacopo del Casentino with *St. Miniato and eight*

183

San Miniato al Monte — Interior.

scenes of his life; the mosaic in the apse represents *Christ enthroned between the Virgin, St. Miniato and the symbols of the Evangelists* (1279, but restored in 1491 by Baldovinetti). From the presbytery one proceeds right into the **Sacristy**, frescoed after 1387 by Spinello Aretino with *Stories of St. Benedict*; the door to the right of the Sacristy leads into the Cloister, with the remains of frescoes by Andrea del Castagno and, in the loggia above, by Paolo Uccello. Back in the church, the so-called **Chapel of the Cardinal of Portugal**, one of the most elegant creations of the Florentine Renaissance, by Antonio Manetti (1461-66), a pupil of Brunelleschi, is off the left aisle; it contains the tomb of Jacopo di Lusitania, archbishop of Lisbon, by Rossellino; fine della Robbia terracottas on the vault, a splendid *Annunciation* by Baldovinetti (on the left) and two *angels* frescoed by Antonio and Piero del Pollaiolo (on the wall at the end, above the copy of the *Saints Eustace, James and Vincent* by the Pollaiolo brothers which is now at the Uffizi).

To the right of the church is the **Bishop's Palace** (13th-14th century). Round the church are the walls of the Fortress erected by Michelangelo in 1529 to defend Florence during the siege by the Imperial troops. During the last century the area surrounded by Michelangelo's fortifications was used as a Cemetery (*Cimitero delle Porte Sante*) and is still in use. It contains the tombs of various famous personalities such as Collodi, author of Pinocchio.

The Belvedere Fortress.

Viale Galileo — Our drive continues from Piazzale Michelangelo along the Viale dei Colli, here called Viale Galileo. On the left are charming villas set in landscaped parks. On the right are stretches of neat fields with the city as a superb background. The whole landscape is dotted with the tall dark-green cypress trees typical of the Tuscan countryside. About a mile from Piazzale Michelangelo we turn right into Via San Leonardo, a picturesque little country road which leads to Forte Belvedere. If, however, we continue down Viale Galileo, we soon come to Piazzale Galileo, the continuation of which is Viale Machiavelli, the last stretch of the Viale dei Colli. Viale Machiavelli winds its way through pleasant parks and gardens, descending to Porta Romana which, leads us back into the centre of Florence.

Via San Leonardo — This is one of the most charming country roads in the vicinity. Along the flagstoned road, you can see the grey-green olive trees peeping above the old stone walls and lovely villas, surrounded by the typical vegetation of the Tuscan countryside. Halfway down, on the right, is a charming Romanesque church, **San Leonardo in Arcetri**, which contains 14th century Tuscan school paintings and a Romanesque *marble pulpit*, (early 13th century). The road ends at Forte Belvedere. Continuing through the San Giorgio Gate (1324), a short walk downhill takes you back to the centre of town.

Forte Belvedere — The building was built between 1590 and 1595 for Ferdinando I de' Medici, by Giovanni de' Medici and Bernardo Buontalenti. Its ramparts command a superb view of the city. Important art shows and other cultural events are periodically held here.

Fiesole – Piazza Mino da Fiesole.

FIESOLE

This charming hilltown (ca. 950 feet above sea level), that entrances Florentines and sightseers alike, was originally founded by the Etruscans. The five mile drive to reach the town from Florence is an experience in itself – as we climb amidst splendid villas and country houses set in a superb Tuscan landscape of cypresses and olive groves, Florence appears beneath our gaze from a different position at every curve.

San Domenico of Fiesole – This picturesque town is halfway up the hill. It was named after the monastery of San Domenico erected here in the 15th century. The church on the main road has a 17th century façade by Matteo Nigetti. Inside are several fine paintings including a *Virgin and Child with Saints* by Fra Angelico (who spent his youth here before moving to the monastery of San Marco in Florence), a *Crucifixion* by followers of Botticelli, and other work by Lorenzo di Credi, Sogliani, to mention only a few. In the Chapter Room of the monastery is a *Crucifixion* by Fra Angelico (c. 1440).

Fiesole — The Praetorian Palace, now the Town Hall.

Turning left opposite the church, a five minute walk takes us to the **church of the Badia Fiesolana** which was the cathedral of Fiesole until 1208. In 1466 it was rebuilt, along with the adjoining monastery, in the Brunelleschian style. The typically Romanesque green and white 12th century façade is set into a bare 15th century front that was never finished. The simple interior is harmonious and effective, reflecting the Brunelleschian influence.

Returning to the main road, we continue our climb until we reach the main square of Fiesole, Piazza Mino da Fiesole.

Piazza Mino da Fiesole — The square is on the site of what was once the Roman Forum. Opposite, on the east side, the building decorated with coats-of-arms is the **Palazzo Pretorio**, now the Town Hall, erected in the 14th century. To the right is an old chapel, the **Oratorio di Santa Maria Primerana**, extensively restored, with a 17th century façade. Inside the building are 14th century frescoes and other interesting works. The *equestrian monument* opposite the Town Hall representing the first King of Italy, Victor Emmanuel IInd meeting *Garibaldi at Teano* is by Oreste Calzolari (1905).

The Cathedral — Consecrated to St. Romulus, the building was begun in 1028 and later enlarged in 1256 and 1300. The whole building, façade, back, and sides, is in plain stone, the overall effect of which is both harmonious and simple. The picturesque crenellated clock-belltower dates from 1213. The interior is typically Romanesque, with a raised choir and lowered crypt and a plain raftered ceiling. The columns along the nave came from Roman buildings. On the main altar is a *Virgin and Child with Saints* by Neri di Bicci. The apse is frescoed with *scenes of the life of St. Romulus* by Nicodemo Ferrucci. To the right of the choir is the **Cappella Salutati** containing frescoes by Cosimo Rosselli (15th century) and two of Mino da Fiesole's finest works: the *tomb of Bishop Leonardo Salutati*, with a bust of Salutati, and the *altar front with the Virgin and Saints adoring the Child* (1464). The *altar* and the *statues of St. Romulus and St. Matthew* in the chapel to the left of the choir are by Andrea Ferrucci (1493).

187

Fiesole — The Roman Theatre: *below*: **Roman portraits of Lares** (Archaeological Museum).

The Roman Theatre — You enter the archeological zone from the little road behind the apse of the Cathedral. In the **Faesulanum Museum** are objects excavated in digs carried out in this area. There are Etruscan tombs, architectural fragments, Etruscan and Latin inscriptions, coins, bronze, and even objects from the Barbarian period and late Middle Ages. Three of the highlights are an Etrusco-Greek statuette of *Hercules*, an Etruscan *mirror with the Sacrifice of Polyxena*, and a *portrait bust of the Emperor Claudius*. The typically-Greek plan theater was discovered in 1792 and excavated in 1873. It was built at the time of Sulla (Ist cent. B.C.), although it was later enlarged under Claudius and Septimius Severus (2nd-3rd century A.D.). Clearly visible is the horseshoe-shaped auditorium with 19 rows of stone benches divided into three sections.

By way of the road going along the west side, we reach the *Etrusco-Roman temples*. On the right are the remains of an Etruscan gate and wall.

188

Fiesole – The road leading up to the monastery of San Francesco; *below*: the church and monastery of San Francesco.

The Bandini Museum – The museum contains 15th-16th century della Robbia terracottas, as well as 14th-15th century paintings. The collection includes works by major artists, such as Ambrogio Lorenzetti, Nardo di Cione, etc.

The Church of San Francesco – To reach the church, one climbs up the steep little lane to the left of the Bishop's Palace. From the terrace at the top of the hill one can enjoy a breathtaking bird's eye view of Florence and the countryside spread out beneath ones feet. There are some interesting paintings inside the Gothic-style church and the monastery contains a charming cloister and a Missionary Museum.

INDEX